Stories of the Heart

Journey into Dying and Living

Stories of the Heart

Journey into Dying & Living

Jim Brulé   Rebecca Claire Lemaire

Stories of the Heart
© 2024 Jim Brulé & Rebecca Claire Lemaire

All Rights Reserved.
Reproduction in whole or in part without the author's permission is strictly forbidden. All photos and/or copyrighted material appearing in this book remain the work of its owners.

Book designed by Erin Lovelien
Front & Back design by Erin Lovelien
Edited by Erin Lovelien

Published in the USA by Fishtail Publishing LLC
www.fishtailpublishing.org
Columbus, Ohio

ISBN: 978-1-7375080-7-6

To my granddaughters - Jim

To all who are suffering and grieving right now, and to all who love stories - Rebecca

Table of Contents

Acknowledgments ix
Introduction xi
A Word On Retelling xvii

Grief and Loss 1
    Death, Vultures, and Humans 3
    The Widow of Ephesus 7
    Bruriah 13
    Leaves from the Garden of Eden 17
    The First Tears 21

Facing Our Own Death 25
    King Sulayman and Azrael 27
    Death's Messengers 31
    The Old Woman and Death 35
    The Stream 43

Historic Grief 47
    The Vow 49
    Tarvaa 55
    Ocean of Tears 59
    The River Olu 65
    The Tear Jar 69

(Im)mortality 73
    The Camel Driver 75
    The Master of the Garden 81
    The Reincarnated Maggid 87
    The Siddha and the Jnani 91

Acknowledgments

I have been accompanied and led on this journey by too many to name, but I want to particularly thank my co-author, Rebecca Lemaire; our publisher, editor, and graphic designer, Erin Lovelien; the treasured faculty of Transformational Storytelling: Maja Bumberák, Hears Crow, and Valentina Ortiz; and my colleagues in this experience, Bill Redfield and Jana Biesanz. I learned so much from the students of our "Journey into Dying and Living" series, who brought their open hearts and minds to this sacred work. And finally, stories would not be what they are to me today without the loving infusion of my mother, Sally Brulé; my teacher, Reb Maggid Yitzhak Buxbaum, zt"l; and my wife, Jill, and family, who are always ready to listen and support my work.

Jim Brulé

There are many people I thank for their direct and indirect contributions to this book, but my gratitude goes first and foremost to my mother and my father. They each, in their own ways, introduced me to the art of storytelling; my father told me many stories of his wild adventures as a child in the Belgian countryside during and after the Second World War while my mother read us stories at night using her best voices and expressions, keeping us in awe and suspense. As I accompanied them on their journeys towards death, they both taught me once again how to live and die in a full and fearless way, influencing the work I do with storytelling, death and grief. I am also deeply grateful to my siblings, as we were able to come together and support my parents and each other in their last moments. I thank the participants on our series 'Journey into Dying and Living' and other sessions I lead in Spain, as their heartfelt responses and sharing have contributed to the development of the stories in this book and my trust in the wisdom found in these tales. I thank my teacher, Numancia Rojas, who died in 2021 and supported me for three years as I started my journey as a professional storyteller. I thank Erin Lovelien for her invaluable help and support in making this book possible. Last but not least, I am full of gratitude for Jim Brulé, my co-author, who reached out to me a few years ago and initiated our collaboration which has been a joy and has taught me more than I can express.

Rebecca Claire Lemaire

Introduction

In many modern cultures and societies, death is surrounded by an aura of taboo. People are often uncomfortable talking about and planning for their dying. Death often feels like a failure, and the efficacy of medical interventions is commonly measured by people's lifespan rather than their quality of life. Grieving is almost always seen as something to get over, fix, or complete; people speak about "overcoming grief" or "obtaining closure" at the death of another.

We do not understand death as such. We see death as an integral part of life rather than its opposite, in the same way that birth or sleep are a part of life. The stories in this book and the questions accompanying them are intended to encourage an exploration of death that embraces its challenges and opens one to its gifts.

As storytellers, we are grateful for the opportunity to have engaged with a wide variety of cultures, a benefit amplified by the tremendous challenges of the pandemic. We decided to select stories from that broad range, expecting that the diversity of cultural perspectives would further enhance the chances of you—the reader—developing a fresh perspective. Our criterion was to select the stories from our repertoire that touched us and fit within the four sections of this book without striving to achieve other balances, such as the gender or ethnicity of protagonists.

While these stories may not always represent our deepest feelings and opinions about the subject of dying and living, they speak to our souls and, hopefully, yours. We will mention below how different interpretations at different times and by different people, and disagreement with or dislike of the stories, may add to their value.

Each of the eighteen stories in this volume is at the core of our four-part course, 'A Journey into Dying and Living,' the subtitle of this book. This means that participants worldwide have encountered each of the stories, which, as storytellers know, evolve and vary with each telling. Throughout our courses, we have the privilege of witnessing the healing power of these stories when we truly engage with them through reflection, discussion, or creative responses.

'A Journey into Dying and Living' points to the idea that, by exploring Death, we inevitably contemplate Life and how we want to live our own. Ultimately, through the exploration and contemplation of Death, we believe that the essence of our being—the Heart of who we are—may be revealed.

Who Is This Book For?

As an individual, you may be searching for solace and understanding during periods of grief, you may be looking for ways to support a loved one through their own experience of loss, or you may want to engage in the contemplation of death more generally as a fact of life. These stories and the accompanying questions can help provide perspective and momentum.

As a group engaged in the exploration of death, you may want to use this book as a structure for discussions about dying and living. The stories and accompanying questions may be used in various ways, of which we give suggestions below.

As a caring professional, you may mine some of these stories and questions for use in your close work with others, accompanying them in their grief or into the journey of death.

As a storyteller, we expect you will find these stories to be rich gems in your repertoire. See our section, 'A Word on Retelling,' at the end of this chapter.

INTRODUCTION

We believe there is no single perspective from which Dying and Living should be viewed. Therefore, we have selected stories from multiple traditions to give the reader a chance to experience a variety of cultural perspectives. This means that no particular spiritual or religious tradition is needed to benefit from these stories, nor should they conflict with any particular tradition.

In short, **if you are ready to open up to the mysteries of living well by acknowledging your mortality, this book is for you.**

Structure

During the course of our work together as oral storytellers leading groups through 'A Journey into Dying and Living,' we explore four themes. The stories related to these four themes have been collected into four sections of this book.

You will quickly notice that the stories in any section resonate with at least one of the other themes. Nonetheless, we have sorted them into these sections and placed them in an order that we believe improves their accessibility. However, you, the reader, are welcomed—in fact, encouraged—to skip around and find the stories that call out to you.

The section on **Grief and Loss** approaches not only the loss of a person but also the many losses we encounter in life—the loss of a relationship, a job, or a dream. Its stories highlight the importance (or not) of ceremony, the thin veil that separates the dead from the living, the gifts that come from loss, and holding room for joy in the midst of grief, allowing for all emotions in their own time. Five stories are found in this section, encompassing European and African sources, as well as Jewish scripture and folklore.

Facing Our Own Death contains stories that point to our possible fear of death and to the 'little deaths' of life and how we might embrace these as a practice for the 'final' death. Of course, every transformation is a kind of death, which encourages us to ask, 'What is it that dies?

What continues?' Typical of our approach, these stories spring from multiple sources, including cultures in Ireland, Appalachia, Germany, and Sufi and Jewish traditions.

The five stories in the **Historic Grief** section encourage us to explore the legacy of our ancestors (which can be viewed metaphorically as painful stones and beautiful jewels) and what use we make of them in our lives. These stories invite us to consider the actions we may take based on ancestral grief. We believe that acknowledging historic grief gives us the opportunity for a new energy and purpose in life. These stories hail from Mongolia, the Yoruba people, and various Jewish cultures.

The fourth section, **(Im)mortality**, explores more deeply that which dies and that which does not. The stories illuminate the eternal and the temporal and question whether they are truly separate. These stories spring from Armenian, Indian, Arabian, and Jewish sources.

One or more questions accompany each story to help explore its content more deeply. Suggestions for engaging with these prompts will be given in the 'How to Use this Book' section below. We also briefly include our sources with each story.

Style

In writing these stories, we have strived to find a balance between a literary and oral storytelling style. Our intention is that the stories be easily readable while retaining the rhythm, simplicity, and straightforwardness of oral storytelling, leaving room for the reader to engage in their own imagination.

How To Use This Book

As humans, stories have the ability to help us move down from our mind to our heart—from our intellect to our soul. The Stories of the Heart are prompts for investigating and exploring our current feelings

INTRODUCTION

and emotions about different aspects of death and loss.

Each story is accompanied by one or more questions, which you will find at the end of the story. These are the types of questions we put to the participants during our sessions, encouraging them to engage with the prompts through free-flow writing, poetry, movement (with or without music), drawing, or discussion. We encourage you to approach these questions in whichever way you feel is right at the time of reading the story. Our suggestions are just that, suggestions.

In the same way, you may want to ignore the questions and suggestions below the stories and engage with a story differently. The stories contain room for multiple understandings and meanings. You might even read or listen to the same story at different times and understand it differently.

You may also finish a story feeling you have not quite understood it. In this case, we invite you to allow the story's mystery to rest within your heart. You may want to write down the questions you have for the story and revisit them upon another reading later on.

Moreover, a story's elements may disturb, annoy, or challenge you. Strong reactions to or not liking a particular story are welcomed. Again, let the unease with the story rest within you, write about it, and see if you can formulate your questions. You may want to discuss it with the group you are working with. Here are some of the questions you might ask yourself:

- What values do I find disturbing in this story?
- What do I wish had happened differently?
- What questions in my life arise as I encounter this story?
- What problems does the story address that I recognize in my life?

You could also read or listen to a story and do nothing with it at first. Some Sufi masters suggest going away after listening to stories and seeing which ones keep coming back to your mind and heart in the next days and nights, maybe even during sleep. You might then want to explore this story further.

As you may have gathered from the above, this is not a book about how to "fix" or do away with grief or the pain and fear of facing death. When we think grief is only to be eradicated, we cut ourselves off from a rich source of truth. Grief can be recognized as a companion throughout our lives, with its own seasons and powers. Sometimes, a helpful approach is to find the beauties of life to walk alongside our grief, softening its hard edges and welcoming the light of our Being to shine through and within. In the same way, by exploring our fear of death, the pain of its inevitability, and the loss of life, some of the difficult emotions may dissolve, or we might simply become aware of the Light that accompanies them, that shines through them. Exploring Death and lifting its veil may lead you to new realizations of Life and the Essence of your Being.

A Word On Retelling

These stories have been told for many generations through the oral tradition. Subsequently, no one owns them, and you are welcome to tell them in your own words and style.

If you do tell them, an acknowledgment of our book would be appreciated, in the same way that we have mentioned our sources—both in respect for other storytellers and to encourage you to create your own versions of these stories.

One of the delights of retelling a story is adapting it to the particular audience to whom it is being told. However, when the story comes from a different culture, special care must be taken not to inadvertently lose cultural referents or impose your own values. Doing so diminishes the culture from whom the story is taken and robs you of the opportunity to encounter a new perspective. Thus, when contemplating making changes to a story from a different culture, we strongly encourage you to do your research, knowing that doing so will almost certainly lead you to new insights!

Jim Brulé
Rebecca Claire Lemaire
October 2023

Grief and Loss

Death, Vultures, and Humans
A Story of the Serer People in West Africa
Retold by Rebecca Claire Lemaire

Long ago, when the gods and goddesses were creating Earth, they made the mountains, the rivers, the lakes, the grass, the trees, the animals, and the humans. Finally, so that they could rest, they made it possible for creatures on Earth to reproduce.

However, after some time, the gods and goddesses looked down and realized that Earth was losing its balance! There was more and more of everything. Too much of everything. The number of plants, animals, and humans kept growing...endlessly. Earth would not be able to carry them all for much longer. What would happen? Even the gods and goddesses did not know. Would Earth tip over if they did nothing?

They discussed and deliberated until, finally, one of the gods had the idea of introducing something called 'Death.'

"Interesting idea," the others replied. "This might solve the problem." They agreed to test the idea on one species first: vultures. They looked down, found a group of vultures, chose one, aimed, and...dead!

When the other vultures in the group realized that their friend was not going to wake up, they screamed, they flew around erratically, they screeched, and they cried for one day, two days, three days, one week, two weeks, three weeks and more. Their screams, cries, and tears did not stop. "This is not going to work," one of the goddesses said. "I agree," replied another. "Their screams and madness will throw the whole world into chaos!"

"This 'Death' experiment might not be the solution, after all! It is just too much for the creatures on Earth," they all agreed.

However, after more brainstorming, deliberations, and discussions, the idea of 'Death' still seemed to be the best one, so they decided to try it on one more species: humans. They looked down, found a group of humans, chose one, aimed, and...dead! When the other humans saw that their friend was not going to wake up, they screamed, they ran around erratically, they wailed, and they cried for one day, two days, three days...

To the gods' surprise, on that third day, amidst the tears, a human picked up a drum and started beating it—crying and drumming. Another person then began to sing—crying, drumming, and singing. The wails and cries turned into songs; love songs for their dead friend. Some people started moving and dancing to the music—crying, drumming, singing, and dancing. That evening around the fire, by the corpse, the humans told stories about that person's life and their beauty in all its forms: their quirkiness, their joys, and their difficulties. Salty tears mingled with sweet smiles and laughter, and gradually, the hard edges of pain softened. The loss of their friend became bearable.

Humans had invented 'Art.'

Seeing what was happening on Earth, the gods and goddesses decided that Death would work after all.

It is since that day that Death exists on Earth.

And it is since that day that vultures, as soon as they see a corpse, eat it up so they don't have to look Death in the face.

And it is since that day that we humans have art, creativity, and ceremony to help us grieve and mourn our dead.

Question
We use this story in our sessions to spark a conversation about ceremony and art in mourning. How can you honor, celebrate, and create a ceremony for whom (or what) you are grieving, right now? You may want to write a poem, sing a song, light a candle in front of a picture or find another creative way to answer this question and mourn your person or situation.

Sources
There are different versions of this story with one God or multiple gods, which you can read and listen to on the Internet, usually in French. Michela Orio, an Italian storyteller living in France, has a beautiful telling on a French radio programme: 'Le Conte est Bon.' Another version is part of a collection of 'Contes Sérères' collected by Raphaël Ndiaye and Amadou Faye.

The Widow of Ephesus
A Roman Story
Retold by Rebecca Claire Lemaire

The woman felt the hard, cold, stone floor beneath her back. She opened her eyes but couldn't see anything; it was pitch dark. She sat up. Then, as her eyes grew accustomed to the darkness, she saw the stone walls around her, the four uneven steps leading up to the door on the right, and next to her, on the left, on a platform, a corpse wrapped in a shroud. She remembered now. Her dear husband had left her...he'd gone ahead without her...he'd been taken away from her!

She now remembered the funeral and the procession. She'd followed her husband's body in the streets of Ephesus, wailing, crying, and beating her chest, as was customary during Roman times; this was expected of a widow. However, as they entered the cemetery and took her husband into the mausoleum, she went beyond what was expected. She declared that she was going with her husband...going with him into the mausoleum, going with him into.... At first, she didn't utter the words. Then, she said she was going to hold vigil and would not eat or drink until she, herself, followed him into death and reunited with him. Some people said she was making a scene, that it was too much. Others, that it was commendable, an example to follow. Everyone expressed an opinion, but she didn't care. She sent them all away angrily.

When alone, at last, she sat next to her husband's body in the shroud.

She sighed
She cried
She wept
She cried some more.
She asked, "Why me?" "Why him?" "Why so soon?"

She then collapsed, and the world went black.

"How long ago was that?" she now wondered. "One day? Two days? More?" She felt dizzy. She tried to get up, but she couldn't; her legs wouldn't carry her. She slowly crawled up the four steps to the door and pushed it open. In the moonlight, she could see the silent cemetery with its tombstones and mausoleums, and there in the middle, like a shadow, rising towards the moon, a cross with a corpse hanging on it.

She heard footsteps approaching, and a young man appeared. He was wearing a soldier's uniform. He looked down at her and said, "Madam, you are not supposed to be here. The cemetery is closed! What are you doing here?"

"I am holding vigil for my husband," she answered abruptly. "Why are you here if the cemetery is closed?"

"I am guarding the thief on that cross," he said. "I am to make sure his family doesn't come to get his body to give him a proper burial."

He lowered his head, and his voice softened as he added despondently, "Orders from the higher authorities. They want to make an example of him."

Then, looking down into her face, he frowned, "Madam, you don't look very well," he said gently. "I have some bread and water back at the cabin and..."

"No! I am fasting until I die!" she interrupted.

She fell silent. Her body ached. Her head was pounding. Dying was not as straightforward as she'd first thought. She was not quite sure *what* she'd imagined; maybe that she'd lose consciousness and never wake up. That would have been easy. Instead, this pain. She wanted to lie down and sleep next to her husband, but she was not sure if she could even make it back down the steps into the mausoleum. She looked at the soldier and said, "Alright then, I'll have just a little bread and water so I can go back and hold vigil." She paused, then added, "And continue to fast until I die!"

As the young soldier ran off to the cemetery entrance to get the food, she turned and faced the inside of the dark mausoleum. She sat silently. She felt numb.

The soldier came back and sat next to her on the top step, leaving the door slightly open so the moonlight shone dimly upon them. She took a sip of the water he'd brought for her. Its freshness felt like a balm for her parched body and soul. As she took a second sip, he told her about how he'd come to the city to look for a job, and how he sent money to his mother back in the village every month. As he chatted away, she picked up the bread he'd placed next to her and ate one little piece at a time, chewing slowly.

Suddenly, the soldier jumped up and said he had to leave. "It'll be dawn soon," he said. "My shift is almost over and if my replacement finds me in here, not guarding the thief on the cross, I'll get into trouble."

The young soldier left, and the woman went back down the steps into the mausoleum. She sat next to her husband's body.

She sighed
She cried
She slept and
She wept.
She asked, "Why me?" "Why him?" "Why so soon?"

She spent the whole day there without eating or drinking.

The following night, the soldier appeared in the doorway. "I've brought you some soup and bread," he said. Once again, they sat beside each other on the top step. She ate some bread and sipped some soup. She sighed. The soldier asked her, "Tell me about your husband. What was he like?" She told him they'd been engaged since childhood, and that their companionship had been wonderful.

"We used to laugh a lot," she said. "I don't feel like laughing now." She also told him how her husband always said that he wanted to take care of her in life and in death. And he'd done so. He'd left all his affairs in order and she could now live comfortably for many years. "But I don't want to live. I don't know *how* to live without him."

The soldier tried to comfort her, but she answered, "You can't understand. You just can't."

So, they sat in silence. Before dawn, the soldier quickly left before his replacement came, and she went back down the steps and held vigil over her husband.

She sighed
She cried
She slept and
She wept.

And so it was. The soldier would come at night. He'd share his food with her. They would sit on the top step, and they would talk or sit in silence. Sometimes, she wept, sometimes, she smiled. Sometimes, she felt numb. During the day, she would go back and sit with her husband, and sigh, and cry, and weep, and sleep.

One night, he brought her some flowers, "To sprinkle your grief with a little beauty," he said softly. Together, they placed the flowers on and around her husband's body.

The next day, more than once, sitting inside the dark mausoleum, she wondered what time it was, *Was it almost nighttime?* Eventually, she climbed the steps and pushed the door open just a little so as not to be seen. The sun was low. *Almost dusk*, she thought, and smiled almost imperceptibly. She then allowed herself to sit there in the doorway and let the sun caress her face just for a moment before going back down to her husband.

The next day, after the soldier had gone, she did the same, and spent more time on the top step, listening to the sounds of the cemetery with her face in the sun rays that shone through the slightly opened door. She was gazing at the white clouds in the sky and the blue spaces between them when she suddenly felt herself 'enter' one of those spaces, so to speak, and there it was: the open, wide open, spacious blue sky....

That night, the seventh night since she had entered the mausoleum, the soldier appeared with food, and—this time—with some wine, too. "It'll warm your heart a little," he said gently. They sat in their usual place, ate, and sipped the wine slowly. She told him about the open blue sky and how her broken heart might also be an open heart. She said that at some point, she would be ready to leave the mausoleum and go home, but not quite yet. The soldier lifted his cup of wine and said, "To not dying yet." "To not dying yet," she answered simply.

And, after a while, "Come," he said. "Let's go and see the stars and the moon." They got up. He pushed the door open, stepped out into the graveyard and, immediately, he noticed! Stunned, he turned around and said to her in a panic, "The body! It's no longer on the cross! The thief is gone! The family... the family must have come and got him," he stuttered. "The authorities won't forgive me! I am going to end up on that cross in his stead. Oh!...what am I going to..."

"Wait! Be quiet!" she said gently but firmly. She turned and looked down at her husband's body lying inside the mausoleum. She then looked back at the soldier. He immediately understood. "What? We can't do that!" he sputtered. "We can!" she answered gently. "I think he would have wanted that," she said. "And I, well...I would rather surrender the dead than slay the living."

The soldier, sweating profusely, stuttering his agreement and disagreement all at once, finally answered, "Okay." Although, his answer sounded more like a question. The woman lifted her cup of wine and said, "To Life!" "To Life," said the soldier with a weak smile.

The pair managed, somehow, to hoist the husband's body onto that cross and replace the thief. Just before dawn, they stood there beneath the cross, tired and covered in sweat, and the soldier looked at the woman. "Thank you," he said in a choked voice. "Thank you!"

The woman looked up at her husband's body on the cross, "Thank you," she whispered. "Thank you!"

Then, the soldier and the widow made their way to the gates of the cemetery. "To Life," they both said, looking into each other's eyes.

They parted.

The soldier walked westwards, and the widow walked eastwards toward the rising sun.

Question
Close your eyes, imagine you are in the mausoleum. What or who is in the shroud for you right now (this could be a person or a situation, anything you feel the loss of)? Sit with this for a while, then put your timer on for 7 minutes and do a free-flow writing exercise starting with, "In the shroud is...."

Sources
I first heard this story told by the wonderful Daniel Morden on Daniel Allison's podcast, *House of Legends*. My research leads me to believe that this story was first found in the Phaedrus in 370 BC. It has been retold and re-written by many authors and playwrights throughout time: in the Satyricon (Petronius), in the Lamentationes Matheoluli in the 13th century, by Aesop, by Marie de France, as well as in plays in the twentieth century. Most of these focus on what is seen as the widow's infidelity. My own telling is closest to Daniel Morden's version in the sense that the main focus is on celebrating life. Even though I have told this story many times, and it has evolved and changed over the years, some of Daniel's brilliant phrases and imagery have stuck with me and are still part of my retelling.

Bruriah
A Jewish Story
Retold by Jim Brulé

In Judaism, the Sabbath is the happiest day, and it starts every Friday evening. The Sabbath is when people feel closest to God, to Heaven, to paradise; all that is beautiful and wonderful in life. It is the day when the mundane falls away, and one can live in this wonderful paradise; all work stops. The only thing one is supposed to do on the Sabbath is to experience pleasure and joy.

Bruriah was one of the few truly well-recognized female Jewish scholars from the days of the Talmud. She was married to Rabbi Meir, who was the head of the Sanhedrin—the Jewish Supreme Court. Both of them were independently strong, knowledgeable, and well-respected, but the two of them together were a formidable team; they would challenge each other with intensity and delight. They would argue about this, and they would struggle with that. Many of their discussions were recorded in the Talmud and preserved for millennia; an honor uncommon in those days for a woman.

On Friday evenings, the women light candles to indicate the beginning of the Sabbath. Prayers are said, and the Torah is studied both at home and in the synagogue. This continues until Saturday evening when another candle is lit and then blown out. Only then is the Sabbath over. This closing ritual is called "Havdalah," after which the regular work week resumes.

One Sabbath, Bruriah and Rabbi Meir and their young twin sons welcomed the Sabbath as usual and had a wonderful meal. After the meal, Rabbi Meir kissed Bruriah and the boys and then went to the synagogue to pray and study. Bruriah stayed home with the boys. Later that night, after evening prayers concluded, Rabbi Meir returned. Like every other Sabbath, they had a lovely night together, fulfilling the commandment to make love on the Sabbath.

The next morning, Rabbi Meir headed quickly to the synagogue to pray and study Torah. Bruriah went to the boys' room to wake them up. She stood in the doorway, looking upon her two sons with such joy in her heart. Then it happened: she called to them, but they didn't answer. She thought perhaps they were sleeping heavily today, or maybe they were pretending, so she called them again. When they didn't answer, she knew something was wrong. She leaned over the one closest to her and shook his shoulder. It was so cold! She shook the other boy—cold as well! She wanted to wail, but it was the Sabbath...

She knew one did not mourn on the Sabbath, so she closed the door, stepped back into the living room, and waited for her husband. As usual, he came home at midday, except this time he said, "Bruriah, where are the boys? Why weren't they at the synagogue?"

"What do you mean they weren't there? Of course, they were there."

"No, I didn't see them."

"Oh, they were there...they are there still! Go back and look again."

So, Rabbi Meir left and came back an hour or so later, "They're not there."

"You must have missed them." Bruriah paused, gathering her thoughts. How could she distract him? With a debate, of course. She gathered herself together and said, "By the way, dear husband, I have a question for you. You said before that you should be angry at sinners because they're breaking God's law. You get so angry at sinners, but, husband, I think you've misunderstood. Let's go study the text." In this way, she engaged him in this bit of study, and thoughts of the boys were forgotten.

Oh, how he loved to debate with her, even if she usually prevailed. When they finally finished, he agreed, "Yes, indeed, the Scripture states that one should hate the sin but love the sinner. Thank you, my beloved wife." His heart softened a little more as he thanked her, and it seemed like paradise again.

But then he exclaimed, "You know what? I'm still wondering where those boys are. I must go look for them again."

"Before you go," she said, "I have another question to ask you." She went on and on. Every time he said it was time to go look for the boys, she interjected with another question. Finally, the sun started to set, and it was time for Havdalah. Before he could ask about the boys again, Bruriah insisted, "They'll be home soon. Let's make Havdalah. It's time!"

With that, they began the ritual for ending the Sabbath, which starts with lighting the candle and ends with extinguishing it. Meir seemed to rush through the prayers, his concerns for the boys growing. When the candle was finally extinguished, he turned to Bruriah, demanding, "It is dark now—I have to go find the boys!"

She was not, however, quite ready for him to search. "Husband, husband, just one moment before you go. I have one last question of law for you." His irritation was evident in his clipped response, "Yes, what is it?"

Bruriah inhaled, long and slow. She knew the outcome of this final exchange, but it was critical that Meir reach that same conclusion with conviction. "A very wealthy man approached me some time ago. He asked me to take some precious jewelry and hold it for him. And, really, I can't tell you how beautiful this jewelry is."

Meir's irritation had not abated; this was such a simple case. Where were his boys? His lips tightened, "Right, very clear. What's the question?"

Bruriah took his hand and drew his attention directly to her. Meir didn't notice the softening of her eyes, the first tears threatening to appear. "He approached me and said that he wants the jewelry back, but I don't want to return it! It's so beautiful. I love it—I don't want to give it up!"

Meir's eyes narrowed in confusion—this was such a straightforward matter! "Of course, you must give it up. Where is the subtlety to this question? He loaned you this. He's asked for it back. You must give it back."

Bruriah took his other hand and gazed directly at him. "All right. Are you sure, husband? Are you sure?"

"Of course, I'm sure."

Finally, she turned, led him to the boys' bedroom, and opened the door. The night fell upon them—Bruriah, Meir, and their two sons.

"Oh, dear husband. The Creator gave us these two jewels. But, now, He's reclaimed them."

And together they wept and cried out, and mourned.

Questions
When is it a good idea to try to contain our suffering? What do we risk by doing so?

Source
This is a story from the Jewish tradition. Bruriah is one of a few women quoted as sages in the Talmud. This particular story is a commentary on the Book of Proverbs *(Midrash Mishlei 31)*.

Leaves From the Garden of Eden
A Jewish Story
Retold by Jim Brulé

Long ago, when communities were small, some people lived in the villages, and others lived on farms. On one farm lived a small family: Avraham, the father, Miriam, his wife, and Rina, their daughter. They did more than grow crops; Avraham was known throughout the small community for his excellent care of horses and his great love for them. He would care for them, raise them, heal them, and train them. So, it was to Avraham that people would go whenever there was a problem or they sought another horse. Avraham and his family—and his horses—lived a good life together.

One day, Avraham was walking through the fields when he saw a small figure coming across the top of the nearest hill; a person, someone he didn't recognize. He waved his hand and called out a greeting, but whoever it was didn't respond; they just kept coming slowly toward him. Avraham moved closer to see who it was. Before long, he realized it was a young boy who was not walking steadily; he seemed to be in distress.

Avraham rushed to the boy's aid. He appeared to be about the same age as Rina. The boy was ill and injured, in critical condition. Without hesitation, Avraham picked him up and took him back to the farmhouse, where he and Miriam provided the best care they could. Over the following days, the boy's health slowly improved, and his wounds were well tended to. When he was finally able to speak, he introduced himself as Chaim. He was an orphan with no family, and so Avraham, Miriam, and Rina decided to adopt him into their own.

Slowly but surely, Chaim's strength began to return. Avraham took him under his wing, teaching him how to care for the horses; showing him how to stroke, brush, and feed them. Despite his physical weakness, Chaim showed a deep understanding and natural talent for working with the horses, even surpassing Avraham's abilities. As a result, Chaim and Avraham became partners in caring for the horses, and Chaim became an integral part of the family. He formed a strong bond with Rina; they became great friends, loving each other deeply. This love grew amongst the family and was echoed in Chaim's love of the horses.

Weeks and months went by, but after a year, Chaim fell ill again. Unfortunately, this time his descent was unstoppable. Avraham and Miriam did everything they could, even bringing in healers from the town. But nothing could be done. It was only after a short time of his relapse that Chaim died. The family was heartbroken, especially Rina, who had grown so close to her brother—for that is how she and the family thought of him. Rina's heartbreak deepened, and her own sadness and despair fell heavily upon her.

Soon, she couldn't get out of bed; she just lay there, barely eating or drinking, caught between sleeping and waking. The healers that were brought in for her couldn't do anything. Avraham and Miriam became terrified—would they lose her as well? They would take turns spending the night with her, hoping she would sleep.

It was during one of those nights that Avraham was sitting with her, half asleep himself. As she lay there on the bed, he had a dream—a vision. He looked up in this dream, and there was Chaim, smiling at him, full of health. Avraham knew it couldn't be Chaim, and yet he knew that it was. He called out, "Chaim, what's going on?"

Chaim said, "Oh, Father, dear father. Here I am! I'm in the Garden of Eden! After I died, I was judged on the merits of my life. The work that I did with the horses, Father, what you taught me elevated me so that I was given a seat here in the Garden of Eden. I can't tell you how beautiful it is here. How sweet the air is. How wonderful it feels to walk upon the grass!"

For a moment, Avraham was so taken with joy at what happened to Chaim that he forgot about his daughter. But, then Chaim said, "Father, father, tell me, how are you? How is my mother? How is my sister, Rina?" A tear ran down Avraham's cheek.

"Chaim, she's here. Oh, Chaim, we are so worried—she is heartbroken at losing you." Avraham began to weep now, fully but quietly. "I'm afraid she might be dying soon."

Chaim said, "No! It doesn't have to be that way; wait here." With that, he disappeared. Not long after he returned, his hands full of leaves. "These are leaves from the Tree of Life, here in the Garden of Eden. Take them. Make a tea of them, and they will heal her." Avraham wept even more deeply now, in despair, for he knew this was only a dream. How could such leaves ever make their way to him?

As he woke and lifted his eyes, he saw the bedroom window was open. Rina was still lying on the bed but covered with leaves—leaves of a kind that he had never seen. He reached over and lifted one between his thumb and forefinger, crushing it. "I've never smelled anything like that before!" He leaped up and ran to the kitchen. Miriam, hearing the commotion, hurried into the room. Avraham described what happened; together, they made tea, and they brought it to Rina. Avraham helped her sit up, and Miriam lifted the cup to her lips. Even before she tasted it—as the aroma gently entered her nose—Rina slowly woke and smiled faintly, then opened her lips to take a sip.

As Chaim predicted, Rina began to heal; it was only a matter of days before she was back to life and brighter than ever. Word of her healing spread through the village like leaves before the wind. Avraham, Miriam, and the entire village rejoiced and gave thanks.

When Rina grew old enough to marry, she married a fine man from the village. And when their first child arrived, they named him Chaim.

Question
The leaves have an aroma, much like memories. Which memories of your departed bring sweetness and healing to you?

Source
This is a story from the Jewish tradition, which I first encountered retold by Howard Schwartz in "Leaves from the Garden of Eden." He gives the source as *Nifla'ot ha-Tzaddikim (Wonders of the Holy Ones)* (Piotrkow, 1911).

The First Tears
A Story from Kabylia
Retold by Rebecca Claire Lemaire

Long ago, when Earth was still fresh and new and humans had recently arrived, they say that tears did not exist. Humans, plants, and animals lived in peace and harmony; they talked to each other and understood each other. However, one day, the humans decided they were more skilled and capable than the plants and animals. They thought that they could dominate nature, perhaps even dominate one another. They stopped talking to the birds and trees, they stopped talking to the animals, and, more importantly, they stopped listening. Envy and jealousy grew, humans tried to enslave each other, and hatred settled in. Eventually, war broke out.

One day, not long after the beginning of the war, a little boy was orphaned. They say he was the first orphan on Earth. He wandered the land alone and abandoned because the other human beings were too deep in their own pain and grief to notice him. Despite his pain, the little boy did not cry because tears did not yet exist.

One night, he was walking across an empty field—alone as usual—and the loneliness and sorrow bottled up inside him was just too much. He felt as though he might explode into a thousand pieces, like the stars above. The lump in his throat was more painful than ever. Unbeknownst to him, up in the sky, the moon was looking down. She saw his pain, she felt his grief, and she decided to help. She slowly floated down through the sky until she came and landed before him. The little boy looked up in awe at the great Being hovering before him. He wanted to greet her but, still choked by sadness, he was unable to say a word. The moon looked at him kindly and said tenderly, "I can see your sorrows and the pain inside you, my young friend, but I've come to tell you there is something else inside you: a river. On that river, you may let the pain and heartache travel out. Let the river out through your eyes, my young friend! Cry, my young friend!"

The orphan tried to feel the river but couldn't. He tried to cry, but he did not know how. The moon gently came closer and held the boy tightly against her. Soon, the little boy felt the river deep down inside him. Hugged by the moon, he felt the river rising, welling up, passing through his chest, his throat, and filling his face. His chin began to tremble, and then it happened: the river reached his eyes. There were just a few tears at first. Then, a trickle that ran down his cheeks, and, finally, the river flowed out freely.

In the moon's embrace, the young orphan boy cried and cried some more, the river shaking his body as it passed through him.

After some time, the river's flow subsided. The boy sobbed. He felt a little lighter. The moon gently released him and asked him how he was feeling. "Better," he said with a weak smile. He could talk now.

The moon reminded him, "You can let this river out whenever you feel it welling up. Now you know how." She added softly, "You must return to the other humans. Tell them about the river. Show them how to cry, my friend."

The boy watched as the moon slowly rose back into the sky. When she was up in her place amongst the stars, shining her light and blessings upon him, he walked toward the villages with a lighter step.

There, in the villages, he told whoever would listen about the moon's gift; the river that was asking to be let out. He taught the humans how to cry. He would look up at the moon, remember her embrace, and share it, putting his arms around whoever found it challenging to let the river out...which was most people. Humans learnt how to cry for themselves and for each other, alone and together. The wars, the pain, and the suffering did not end, but they say that the tears softened the pain, and some compassion returned to the world.

In Kabylia, in the north of Algeria, they say that the patches you see on the moon at night are the marks of the tears from that orphan as he cried for the first time in the moon's powerful yet gentle embrace.

They are the marks of the first tears of humanity.

Dear reader, next time you feel that you can no longer bear the grief, the sadness, and the pain, look up at the moon and remember her gift, remember her words, "Let the river out, my friend! Cry, my friend!"

Questions
Close your eyes, feel the river inside—right now, what is on that river for you? What is no longer needed? What can you ask the river to wash out?

Sources
I thank Isabela Méndez Erminy, a storyteller from Venezuela, for this story, as I heard her share her version at the Munt de Mots International Festival in Barcelona. We connected and exchanged stories. I subsequently found a written version by Jihad Darwiche, a Franco/Lebanese storyteller.

Facing Our Own Death

King Sulayman and Azrael
An Ancient Middle-Eastern Story
Retold by Rebecca Claire Lemaire

'King Sulayman the Wise,' or 'King Sulayman the Kind,' they called him. He was said to have a direct connection with his Creator and all of Creation. Every morning, he would open the doors of his palace to greet his subjects, listen to them, and give them advice if they asked.

One morning, as the audience hall was packed and people were queuing to seek guidance from him, King Sulayman noticed a young man run into the crowded room. In the eyes of this young man, the King saw terror. He waved at him and beckoned him to his presence. The man approached and bowed, breathing heavily. He looked up at the King, who asked gently, "What is this distress I see? What can I do for you?"

"Your Majesty!" answered the man, in a panicked whisper, looking around furtively. "I saw him, in the marketplace, just outside the palace!"

"Who?" asked the King. "Who did you see?"

"Azrael. I saw Azrael, the Angel of Death!" The man's voice broke, "He is here for me. I know so because of the way he looked at me...oh! Your Majesty, that look was so filled with anger! I am young, Your Majesty. I cannot die!"

The King looked down at the man who was trembling and said softly, "Azrael receives his orders directly from God, and he never wavers when it comes to his duty. What can *I* do?"

The young man begged, "I don't know, your Majesty, but they say you are all-powerful. They say you talk to the elements, and...yes! Maybe you could ask the wind to take me away from here? Far, far away! I don't know where, but far...oh! I know...there is a land they call Hindustan. It is at a great distance from here. I would be safe there! Please, Your Majesty—ask the wind to take me there."

The compassionate King found it difficult to refuse the request and accepted with a gentle sigh.

Soon after, the wind came and delicately picked up the man, and the long journey to Hindustan began.

While they were travelling, the man felt the wind whispering something in his ear but, preoccupied with escaping death, he did not pay attention.

Finally, they arrived in Hindustan, and the wind put down the man gently. The man laughed with relief, "I'm alive! I'm safe! I've escaped!"

The next morning, back at King Sulayman's palace in the crowded audience hall, the King noticed Azrael. He called him over and discreetly addressed the Angel, "Why do you scare people like that? Yesterday, you stared at a man in such a way that he became terribly frightened and abandoned his whole life here to flee from you. Why don't you just take people away gently and with compassion? Why did you look at him with such anger?"

"I wasn't angry," whispered the confused Angel. "He misunderstood. I looked at him in surprise, not in anger. You see, Your Majesty, I am supposed to take this man's soul away today. I am to meet him this afternoon, but far, far away from here! So, when I saw him here, in the marketplace, I was perplexed and thought, *Even wearing all the wings in the world, this man could never arrive on time at our meeting place in Hindustan!*"

Questions
What is it about death that you might fear? If you were the young character in this story, and you wanted to go to a safe place, where would you go?

Sources
The origins of this well-known story are unclear. It has traveled far and wide across space and time from Attar to Cocteau. This version is partly based on Rumi's rendering of the story in the *Mathnawi*.

Death's Messengers
A Grimm Story
Retold by Rebecca Claire Lemaire

Long ago, when giants still roamed this earth, one of them was walking down a lane with a spring in his step when suddenly, at a crossroad, a strange 'being' sprang up before him and said firmly, "Halt! Stop! Not so fast, I am here for you!"

The giant looked down at the being and growled, "What? Who are you that you dare speak to me in this fashion? No one says 'Halt' to me."

"I am Death," said the being. "Your time has come." Then, realizing that this was not going to be an easy one, Death added gently but unwaveringly, "No one resists me, you know. You have to come with me now."

However, the giant would have none of it, and when Death approached and wrapped around him to take him away, the giant struggled, wriggled, and broke free from Death's embrace. They wrestled.

"I am not going anywhere!" the giant yelled. "I have things to do!" It was a long and difficult battle. The giant was surprised. This 'being' that had, at first, seemed so small, was all over the place; in front of him, behind him, on top of him, and even inside him. However, eventually, the giant got the upper hand and knocked Death down with his fist, causing Death to collapse.

The giant quickly went on his way while Death lay there, unable to move.

Death worried, "If I don't get up, what will happen to the world? Plants, animals, and humans will multiply without limit. People will become very sick and plead for me to come and get them. Earth will get overcrowded and stagnate…then…end. Oh, no…not this again!" You see, this was not the first time this happened to Death. Death had been ambushed and captured before: tied to a tree, trapped in a nutshell, impeded, and fought with in all sorts of manners. And, each time, the world had been on the brink of collapse. But people—and giants, too—forgot, and history repeated itself.

Death tried to get up again but couldn't.

Just then, a young man walking down the road, saw the half-conscious 'being' lying there. Immediately, he ran to help. He sat on the ground, raised Death's head up gently, and, supporting it on his arm, offered Death water. He then went and got a big leafy branch for shade and held it over the strange being until Death regained some strength. Death felt better and asked the young man, "Do you know who I am? Do you know whom you've helped?"

"I don't," replied the young man. "Have we met before? Should I know who you are?"

"I am Death." And, seeing panic in the young man's eyes, "Don't worry, your time hasn't yet come, but I can spare no one, and I can't make an exception for you. I will have to take you with me when it is your time to go, just like everyone else. However, I would like to thank you for your help. Is there anything I can do for you?"

The young man was already on his feet, backing away. "No, thank you," he stuttered hastily. "I should go now." He turned and hurried off. But, after a few steps, he stopped, turned around, and shouted back.

"Maybe you *could* do something for me!"

"What is it?"

"Could you please give me a warning before you come and get me? I'd like that, so it's not such a surprise, you know?"

"Of course," said Death. "I shall send messengers." And, after a pause, "I usually do." But the young man did not hear this last part. He was far away already.

Death got up and stood there for a while, wondering in which direction the giant had gone. *This is going to be one of those long and tedious pursuits,* thought Death with a sigh. *I'll probably have to fight that giant again before taking him away like everyone else.*

The young man who had helped Death at the crossroad carried on with his life, which was a good one. His encounter with Death had changed something subtle within him. He now lived one day at a time, without fear, cheerful and carefree.

One day, he fell gravely ill, but as he got worse and was bedridden, he kept thinking, *It's alright, I won't die. Not yet. Death promised I would receive a warning or see a messenger.* Indeed, he did not die from that illness. He got better and continued living carefree right into his old age.

Many years later, he was sitting on a bench one day, leaning on his walking stick, smiling and looking at children playing and climbing the trees. He remembered his youth when his legs and knees were strong enough so that he, too, could reach those highest branches.

He felt a tap on his shoulder. He looked around, and there was Death, "It is time to go now, my friend," said Death with a gentle smile. "Come."

"What?" cried the man. "We had a deal! You promised you'd send a warning before you came! Why do you always do that? Why do you always surprise people? You are evil!"

Death looked at the old man with love and compassion, "I *did* send you messengers. Did you not get very ill years ago and lose some of your physical strength? What about the white hair and wrinkles you see in the mirror? How about your memory loss, poor eyesight, and frail bones? I've sent you many of my messengers! I am sorry you did not understand their messages."

Mouth open, the man thought of all the messengers of Death that had come to him during his life.

"And, what about my brother, Sleep?" continued Death. "Has Sleep not reminded you of me? You went with Sleep without resisting every night. Please, come with me in the same way."

The old man who had helped Death all those years ago suddenly felt his shoulders relax. He looked at Death, sitting there, arms wide open and smiling at him. The man smiled back with his eyes, and nodded.

He gently leaned into Death's embrace, the way he had done with Sleep, every night.

Questions
Which messengers of Death have come to you lately? How do you feel about them? How can you embrace them as part of life?

What would it be like to lean into Death's embrace ('final' death or one of the many small deaths of life and changes) as we do with Sleep every night?

Source
This is my version of a famous Jacob and Wilhelm Grimm story. Die Boten des Todes, *Kinder-und Hausmärchen*, (Children's and Household Tales -- Grimms' Fairy Tales), 7th ed. (Berlin, 1857), no. 177.

The Old Woman and Death
A Story That Has Travelled the World
Retold by Rebecca Claire Lemaire

Once upon a time, somewhere in the world—just outside a village—there was a little cottage in which lived an old woman. She'd spent her life picking herbs and plants in the neighboring forest, and with them, she made medicine for the people of the village. She'd also traveled the world, they said, and the villagers often gathered in her house on winter evenings to listen to her stories about those strange, distant lands and their people, with whom the villagers were surprised to have so much in common. She was the oldest in the village, but no one knew exactly *how* old she was because for as long as people could remember, she'd been celebrating her 80th birthday—year after year!

One day, the old woman was dusting and cleaning her living room and singing her favorite song, which she'd learnt somewhere along her travels. She couldn't quite remember the melody or the exact words, but she did remember the first stanza:

> *"Oh, thank you to life,*
> *that's given me so much,*
> *that's given me so much!*
> *Oh, thank you to life*
> *that's given me so much,*
> *that's given me so much!"*

She was singing and dusting, dusting and singing, when there was suddenly a knock on the door. "Already?" she wondered, opening the door. Immediately, she recognized her visitor. "Oh!...Lady Death! I wasn't expecting you today. Er...please come in and shut the door behind you. It's cold outside. Come in, come in...my goodness! You are freezing! Come. This way."

She shut the door behind Death, led her visitor toward the fireplace, sat her down in the armchair, put her feet on a little stool, and said kindly, "There, there, dear. You'll warm up in no time. You'll feel better soon, you'll see!"

Then, she went back to dusting the cobwebs.

> *"Oh, thank you, to life,*
> *that's given me so much,*
> *that's given me so much!..."*

Death recovered from her surprise and got up, walked toward the woman, held her hand out, and said, "Yes, I am Death, and it is time to go now. Come on!"

"Yes, yes, of course," answered the old woman. "But not quite yet! I need to finish cleaning. And, while you're here," the old woman added, "why don't you help me?" She picked up a broom and put it in Death's hands.

"But... I am Death. I do not...sweep!" said Death, looking at the woman in disbelief.

"Oh, it's really easy," said the old woman. "You'll get the hang of it in no time. Just like this, look!" She picked up the broom and showed Death how to sweep. Startled, Death started sweeping the floor as best she could. Then, the old woman said, "Sing with me. When we sing, the work goes much faster."

"But...I am Death. I do not sing!"

"Oh, it's really easy," laughed the old woman. "Just two sentences! You'll get the hang of it in no time."

> *"Oh, thank you to life*
> *that's given me so much..."*

Well, dear reader, if you'd been a little fly on the wall of the cottage that day, you would have witnessed a very confused Death, sweeping and...yes...

singing in a hesitant voice:

> *"Oh, thank you to... life(?)...*
> *that's given me so much,*
> *that's given me so much!..."*

They cleaned the large living room together and, following the woman's instructions, Death helped push the furniture against the walls, creating an open space in the middle of the room. The old woman said, "Perfect! Just the way I want it. Thank you, Lady Death, for your help!"

Death, holding her hand out, said, "Okay, then. It is time to go now. Come on!"

"Yes, yes, of course," answered the old woman. "But not quite yet! I need to finish cooking the meal. Come and help."

"But...I am Death. I do not cook!" said Death. But the woman was already in the kitchen. Mumbling under her breath, Death followed and helped cut the vegetables, mince the parsley, and stir the stew. They brought out the delicious-looking dishes to the living room and put them on the big dining table.

"Fantastic!" said the old woman. "Just the way I want it. Thank you, Lady Death, for your help."

"All right, then," said Death, a little impatiently now, holding out her hand. "It is time to go, now. Come on!"

"Yes, yes, of course," said the old woman, grinning. "But not quite yet! I must get changed." And, just before she went into her bedroom, she turned and added, "While I am changing, would you mind opening the door for the first visitors when they arrive?"

"Visitors?" asked Death in the most high-pitched voice she had ever used.

"Yes, it's my birthday!" answered the old woman.

"Your birthday?" gasped Death.

"Yes, I thought you would know something like that. Every year, the whole village comes to celebrate with me."

She smiled at Death, "Be a dear and open the door for the first guests when they come!"

The old woman disappeared into her bedroom, and Death went toward the front door, muttering, "What next?"

It wasn't long before there was a knock on the door. Death opened. A young couple stood there, and they both let out a cry. "Who...or what...is that?" asked the young man.

"I don't know!" whispered the young woman. "Maybe a long-lost friend of Grandma's? Be polite! I think...I think she's...smiling. It should be fine. Let's go in."

"Smiling?" asked the young man. "How on earth can you see that?" But he followed his wife into the house. He even tried to smile at Death as he brushed past her, trying to keep as much distance as possible between them.

Death closed the door behind the couple.

More guests arrived: the old woman's friends and neighbors, her children, her grandchildren, her great-grandchildren, musicians, and the rest of the villagers.

Some people got very angry at Death opening the door for them, without quite understanding why. Others, burst out laughing. Some ran away, hid behind a tree, and stood in the cold, spying on the house to see what happened to the next guests as they entered. Some people did not even notice Death; they just walked right in...or maybe they *pretended* not to see her.

Soon, the cottage was filled with people. The old woman came out of her bedroom. She was resplendent in a shiny yellow dress and black dancing shoes.

To her confused and concerned guests who were asking her *who*...or *what* the stranger was, she simply answered, "This is Lady Death, and she's going to celebrate with us tonight."

Some people looked at each other, thinking the old woman's tired mind was playing tricks on her. Others smiled. And others, discreetly, moved as far as they could from Death.

The party began; the guests ate and drank, chatted, and laughed, and, gradually, they seemed to get used to Death's presence amongst them. Some even made conversation with her. At one time, she was seen in the kitchen, helping the old woman's granddaughter with placing the candles on the cake. Then, she was sitting by the fireplace, surrounded by all the children of the party, telling them something—a story, perhaps?

After that, the musicians got their instruments out. Of course, they started by playing and singing the old woman's favorite song, and everybody sang along:

> *"Oh, thank you to life,*
> *that's given me so much,*
> *that's given me so much!*
> *Oh, thank you to life*
> *that's given me so much,*
> *that's given me so much!"*

Some could have sworn they heard a deep and ethereal voice at the back, singing along, too....

They sang many songs, then the musicians began to play faster. The old woman approached Death, held her hand out, and said, "Lady Death, come on! Let's dance!"

Death answered, "But...I am Death. I do not..." This time, she did not finish her sentence. She stood up with a sigh and a slight smile. She took the old woman into her arms, and they danced.

It was such a sight that everybody stepped back to watch the old woman whirling and skipping in Death's arms. They danced and danced, faster and faster, until the old woman, out of breath but beaming, said, "Wait, I need to rest!" She looked around, took a young man's arm, and putting his hand into Death's hand, said, "You dance with Lady Death now!"

"No...I can't," started the young man. But, as you may have noticed, it was very difficult to resist a request from the old woman. And so, the young man danced with Death, as did other guests after him, all strongly encouraged by the smiling old woman.

People sang, ate, drank, and celebrated the old woman until dawn, when guests began to leave.

The old woman stood at the door. She gave a hug and a wise and kind word to each one of them. Her neighbors and family held her tightly in their arms. And, when everyone had gone but her closest family, they said to her, "We'll stay. We don't want to leave you alone with...you know...."

But, the old woman answered calmly, "Lady Death is my friend. I am happy to go with her. Go, now. Live well," she said, gently pushing them out the door.

When, finally, she had closed the door behind her last guest, she turned to Death, smiling widely, and said, "Thank you, my dear Lady Death. Thank you for letting me celebrate my last 80th birthday on this Earth!" The old woman offered her open hand to Death and said, "It's time to go now. Come on then!"

Death hesitated, then answered, "Yes, yes, of course! But...not quite yet..."

You see, Death had enjoyed herself so much that night that she asked if she could return the following year to celebrate the old woman's birthday once again!

And so, she did! She danced with more guests and talked to more people from the village. And the year after that, too!

And at the end of that third year's celebration, the old woman closed the door behind her last guest, turned to Death, held out her open hand, and said, "This is it, Lady Death. My body will not manage much longer. It's *really* time for me to go now. Come on, my dear friend!"

Lady Death nodded, and off they went together, hand in hand, smiling and singing:

> *"Oh, thank you to life,*
> *that's given me so much,*
> *that's given me so much!*
> *Oh, thank you to life*
> *that's given me so much,*
> *that's given me so much!"*

To this day, the people of the village still tell this story. They say that since those birthday parties, no one has ever feared Death again. You see, over those three years in which Death came and celebrated with them, every single person in that village, from the youngest to the oldest, got to know Death. Every single person in that village, from the youngest to the oldest, had the opportunity to talk to Death and listen to Death. And by the end of that third year's celebration, every single person in that village, from the youngest to the oldest, had danced with Death!

Question
Imagine you are invited to the party. You knock on the door, and Death opens—right now, what would your reaction be?

Sources
I am eternally grateful to Lyn Ford for introducing me to this story, which became one of my favourites and one I have told numerous times in Spanish, English, and French. Lyn's version is on Youtube: 'Lyn Ford goes spooky.' I recommend listening to it as it is quite different from my version. Lyn told me she heard this story from her family, who are "Affrilachian": people of African American, Native American, and European American heritage. Lyn is including her version of the story in an upcoming book tentatively titled *Grandmothers, Illusions, and Dreams*.

I subsequently found a children's version written by Pascal Teulade, translated from French and published in Mexico, and I have also heard various oral versions based in Ireland.

The words of the song 'Oh, thank you to Life' are translated from and inspired by 'Gracias a la Vida' by Violetta Parra. The melody I sing these words to is my own composition and is accompanied by the kalimba.

The Stream
A Sufi Story
Retold by Jim Brulé

This is a story from the early times, before there were people; when possibilities seemed endless and the horizons were both distant, yet clearly visible. The view from above the world was spectacular—particularly from the highest mountain peak. From that vantage point, ranges and ranges of mountains could be seen and, just beneath that mountain, rocky crags. Beyond those steep cliffs of the mountain, a thin and scraggly forest began. As the slope grew less severe, it became a rich, deep forest. Beyond the forest were meadows and plains, and then more mountains, in a recurring melody of terrain. Until finally, in the distance rested the great ocean.

One day, there was a sudden rumbling and an explosion, and out from the rock burst a spring of fresh, clear, powerful water racing down the mountain. That stream yearned for one thing: the ocean. As it cascaded past boulders, splashing and boiling around rocks, it never lost its yearning. Once it reached the edge of the forest, it could taste the difference in the soil; it could feel the rough bark of the trees as it flowed around them and splashed over their roots.

Lower and lower it traveled, still yearning for the ocean. When the ground began to level, it slowed a little, finding rich earth beneath it—an earth that tasted even more fantastic. Sometimes, the stream took a moment to puddle before moving on, to listen to the birds in the trees. As it flowed into a meadow, the ground grew flatter and it slowed a little more. One thing didn't change: its yearning for the ocean.

Even as it grew wider and slower in the meadow, the stream remained confident of its destination. But then it encountered the unexpected: a desert. At first, it tried to flow across the sand, but it barely made any progress—it was swallowed up! It pulled back and sent out another rivulet, but that was swallowed up, too. No matter what it tried, the desert drank the stream. It couldn't go any further!

The stream stopped and formed a pool as it tried to decide what to do. Realizing it couldn't cross the desert, its yearning grew even stronger, so strong that the grasses in the meadow behind felt it, too. The grasses sighed and the trees on the hillside seemed to moan along in despair, but the stream could see no way to cross this desert.

The desert whispered to it softly, "Come, cross me. You can cross me. You can do it."

The stream knew that this was absurd. "No," it answered. "I've seen what you do—you will drink me up."

"No," the desert replied. "Come—you can cross me. The wind crosses me every day; surely you can, too."

"No, no, I know you. You will just drink me up, and I'll be no more."

Then, the wind appeared and sighed to the stream, "Come, I will carry you across the desert. Come!"

The stream grew angry at the wind's suggestion. "No! I am heavy—I am water; you can't carry me across! You can fly across, but I must flow on top of the desert and would surely be swallowed."

The wind sighed again, "Oh, stream, you have forgotten who you truly are. Come, remember your true essence."

Now, it was confused. "What do you mean?"

"Who are you?" the wind answered.

"I'm... I'm water. I'm living water, with a yearning to get to the ocean!"

"Yes, of course you are. If you yield your vapors to me, I will lift you across the desert, fly you to the far mountains, and deposit you on the cool side so that you can continue your journey."

Now, fear rose in the stream so very strongly. "No! If I yield to you, you'll mix me with other streams and other rivers, and I won't be the same. You'll change me—forever!"

At that, the desert raised her dry voice. "Oh, stream, you will be changed no matter what you do. If you stay here and wait, you'll just become a swamp and will lose your essence. If you find your way to the ocean, you'll be transformed there! The question is, do you remember who you truly are?"

The stream thought, and thought, and realized the truth. It sighed and gave up its vapors, surrendering to the wisdom of the wind and the desert.

Then, it was lifted up and carried for miles and miles across the desert to the far mountains, where it fell like rain on the cool side, mingled with others, but making its way.

Always to the ocean.

Question
As you think about your path through life, what are you yearning for? What slows you down but perhaps brings benefit to yourself and others?

Sources
This story comes from a variety of Sufi sources, most likely originating in the 18th century in oral and written form. It was printed in "Mystic Rose from the Garden of the King: a fragment of the vision of Sheikh Haji Ibrahim of Kerbelam," Sir Fairfax Cartwright (tr), 1899, but was most popularly retold by Idries Shah as "The Sands" in "Tales of the Dervishes," who writes: *This beautiful story is current in verbal tradition in many languages, almost always circulating among dervishes and their pupils. The present version is from Awad Afifi the Tunisian, who died in 1870.*

Historic Grief

The Vow
A Jewish Story
Retold by Jim Brulé

There once was a disciple—a *hassid*—of a great mystic known as the *Maggid* of Kozhnitz. The *hassid* and his wife, Sarah, led very good lives. They kept the Sabbath, they gave to the poor, and they welcomed the stranger into their home; they were truly exemplary. However, they suffered from one unfulfilled dream: to have a child. Each of them felt their lives would be complete if only they could have a child, yet none was coming.

The *Maggid*, like other great mystics, was adept at prayers, potions, and amulets; he knew how to invite blessings upon a seeker. As the wife of one of the *Maggid's hassids*, Sarah would tell her husband to go to the *Maggid* and ask him for some kind of intervention—some kind of prayer or potion—to let them have children. Her husband, though, was reluctant to ask for such a favor. He really didn't want to go and so he kept putting her off.

Each week, she would ask, and each week, he would stall. Finally, she declared that, if necessary, she would visit the *Maggid* herself! Somehow, that was even more embarrassing a prospect, so he agreed to go. He set up a time to meet the *Maggid* that following week.

When the *hassid* arrived to meet with the *Maggid*, he simply poured out his heart, pleading with the *Maggid* to help them to have a child. The *Maggid* paid close attention, and when the request was complete, he bowed his head in introspective prayer. After a long silence, he raised his head, and his brow furrowed in concern.

"I can help you," he said. "But it will involve a tremendous sacrifice for both you and your wife." The *hassid* started to ask, "What sort…" but the *Maggid* waved him into silence. "I cannot be certain. I do know who has the answers, and I do know the first sacrifice. But, beyond that…" his voice trailed off again. "Bring your wife here, and I will explain." The *Maggid* lifted his hand in dismissal, and the interview was over.

Sarah was filled with anticipation, a little fear to be sure, but if the *Maggid* said there was a solution, their dream could be realized! So, they wasted no time in returning. When they arrived, the *Maggid's* wife showed them into his office to wait. Finally, he arrived and began his explanation.

"I do not know what must be repaired; I only know there is a heavy price," he began. "To pay that price, you will each have to throw yourselves into poverty by selling everything you own—saving all the proceeds for the task that will be given to you—and be separated for a great period. You," he turned to Sarah, "will have to go back to live with your family as if you are divorced. And you," turning to the *hassid*, "will have to beg for food and lodging. Only then can your journey begin."

The couple looked at each other, contemplating what had just been described. Slowly, wordlessly, they nodded to each other in agreement and then turned to the *Maggid*. "You must speak your agreement," he announced firmly but caringly. "This is too great a thing to undertake otherwise." Sarah spoke first, "Yes, I will." The *hassid* spoke immediately thereafter, "Yes, I agree."

The *Maggid* nodded and spoke again. "So be it—you have spoken! Here is what you must do. Take all of the proceeds of your sale to the Seer of Lublin, without spending a single kopek of it! Take it all to him, for the Seer of Lublin clearly sees the past and future, and he will have your answer."

It fell upon them, in that moment, what a sacrifice they would have to make. They hadn't been apart since their wedding and, while they didn't have much, they lived a comfortable life. Now, they would have to separate for who knows how long and live without anything; all for a 'cure' that might not work! They looked at one another, searching each other's eyes, holding hands. They both wanted children, but it was such a price! The *hassid* trembled at the magnitude of their undertaking, but Sarah looked at him sternly, whispering, "We made a vow." Slowly, they thanked the *Maggid* and left. Within days, they sold everything they owned and ended up with a purse of 300 pieces of silver—a tremendous amount of money. Sarah went to live with her family, and the *hassid* headed off to Lublin, the words of the *Maggid* ringing in his mind. He traveled by foot, begging for food and shelter. Unable to spend a kopek, he often slept by the side of the road and didn't eat at all; he lost track of the days it took him to get there.

When he finally made it to the Seer's home, he waited patiently to be greeted, but he wasn't—he was relegated to sitting on the ground outside. Other *hassids* came and went, but, day after day, he was never invited inside. He begged for food and drink from passersby, but the invitation to meet with the Seer never came. One day, the Seer's wife looked out as she brought her husband a meal, and saw him. A few minutes later, the door opened for the *hassid*, and the wife showed him to the Seer's office. He sat there in front of the Seer and waited patiently for him to finish reading. Hours seemed to go by until, finally, the Seer looked up at him and said, "I know why you're here. You don't even remember her name, do you?"

The *hassid* was confused. Of course, he knew his wife's name! "What do you mean, Holy Seer? Sarah—of course I know my wife's name—it's Sarah!"

The Seer's eyes narrowed, his voice stern. "Not your wife. I mean Miriam. You don't even remember her name."

It all came rushing back to the *hassid*—Miriam. Miriam was the woman to whom he had been betrothed as a youth but instead of marrying her, he abandoned her. He hadn't even thought of her when he married Sarah. Suddenly, it all became clear. How could they conceive when he was still betrothed to Miriam? How could they conceive when he had broken such an important vow?

The Seer saw an understanding register in the *hassid*, so he explained that the *hassid* must find Miriam. According to the time-honored tradition of forgiveness, the *hassid* must acknowledge his crime and express his genuine regret. He must also repair the damage in whatever way he could, and only then could he ask for forgiveness—which she may or may not grant.

The *hassid* looked at the Seer in despair, "How will I ever repair the damage? How will I ever get her to forgive me? Of course, I will acknowledge my breaking of the vow, but how will I ever find her? It's been so very long…"

The Seer sighed and lifted the book that lay before him, "I understand, but that is your problem." The Seer opened the book in dismissal. As he turned to leave, the *hassid* remembered the silver and coughed slightly. *Was this his fee to be paid to the Seer?* The Seer lifted his eyes momentarily. "No, you will need that," the Seer declared. With that, the interview was over, and the bag of silver felt even heavier in the *hassid's* hand.

As soon as the *hassid* left, he began asking everyone where he might find Miriam, but nobody knew her. It had been so long ago in a different community. Then, he realized that the great fair in Zwolen was only a couple of weeks away. Everyone would be there, and he could make it on time by foot. So, he set off for the fair and arrived on the first day.

The fair lasted for almost a week. Every day, at every moment, he would ask every person if they knew Miriam, but no one did. All the while, he kept the bag of silver intact and didn't spend a single kopek. Instead, he slept in the street, begged for food, and shivered in the occasional rain. On the last day of the fair, the rain came down in buckets. Everyone was driven indoors except one woman off across the far side of the square. She was an elegantly dressed woman, with a maidservant holding an umbrella over her head. *Could that be Miriam?* he wondered. When they were betrothed, they were both so poor. As he approached her, drenched by the rain that came down so hard, he heard her voice, filled with disgust, "There he is. I'll bet he doesn't even remember my name."

The *hassid's* heart had opened in those weeks of fasting and repentance, so it wasn't with joy that he finally reached her but with abject sorrow. He fell to his knees and cried out, "Miriam, Miriam. I've wronged you—so long ago. I've wronged you so badly." She looked down at him, silent, nodding, merely acknowledging the truth that he spoke. "Miriam, I must beg your forgiveness. It started out that I wanted your forgiveness for my wife and me, but…"

Suddenly, she spoke, her words sharp and abrupt, "You married?"

Head bowed, the *hassid* replied, "Yes, I did. It all started out—my seeking your forgiveness—to try to have children. We can't have children because of my broken vow. But, Miriam, I deeply regret this pain, even if we never have children. So, I know I have no right to ask you for this, but please, would you forgive me?"

She looked down at him, his sincerity reaching her. After a long silence, she spoke, her words softened now. "My brother lives a few miles away, and he's come on desperate times. His daughter is ready to be married, but he has no money for the dowry. Go find him, pay the dowry, and I'll know your repentance is sincere. When you pay him, I will forgive you." With that, she turned to her handmaid, and they started to walk away.

The *hassid* let his head fall to the wet earth in gratitude. When he lifted his eyes, she was already gone. He raised himself up and made his way down the road she'd indicated, finally knowing what this sack of silver was for. Two days later, he reached the town and sought out her brother. Everyone knew the brother of Miriam whose daughter couldn't be married. He found him sitting by the side of the road, desolate.

The *hassid* sat down beside him and spoke, "I understand your daughter needs to be wed, but she has no dowry."

The man's gaze turned to him, his eyes filled with pain and scorn. "Yes! Will you mock me, too?"

"No, no!" the *hassid* replied. "I want to help! How much is the dowry?"

"It's 300 pieces of silver, well beyond my means."

The *hassid* raised his bag and said, "By the grace of God, I have exactly that amount with me—and it's yours."

The brother looked at him, confused. "Why would you give that to me? I don't know you—why?"

"I know your sister, and she asked me to give this to you. She asked me to come and pay your dowry."

The brother's confusion grew, "My sister? My sister asked you? Then, what took you so long?"

Now, the *hassid* was confused.

The brother continued, "What took you so long? She's been dead for ten years!"

In that moment, they both heard her voice saying, "I forgive you."

It is known that the *hassid* stayed for the wedding and that he rejoiced with the bride. As for what happened next, that is another story.

Questions
What regrets do we carry? How might we transform them into blessings for others?

Sources
Retold by Howard Schwartz as The Dead Fiancée in "Leaves from the Garden of Eden," Oxford University Press, 2009. He cites several variants of the story which name different locations and prophetic roles.

Tarvaa
A Mongolian Story
Retold by Rebecca Claire Lemaire

This story happened long, long ago, in the distant land of what is now Mongolia, with its lakes, steppes, vast plains and skies, and its unending mountain ranges. One year, a terrible black plague descended upon its inhabitants, and thousands of men and women, young and old, died a relatively quick but very painful death. Whoever got caught in the grips of that plague had no chance of survival.

Those who were still healthy had a choice: they could sit with their sick loved ones, hold their hand, care for them, and accompany them...into death...or, they could flee. Most of them fled. As they ran, they cried out to each other, "We must escape! We must escape! Destiny will take care of the fate of the sick!"

Amongst the sick who were left behind to die was a very young man—still a boy, in fact—named Tarvaa. Young and strong, Tarvaa battled with the forces of death for some days and nights until, exhausted, feverish, and weak, he finally lost consciousness. Soon after, his soul rose above his body and started the long and difficult descent toward the Underworld.

At the end of his perilous journey, he arrived at the gates of the Underworld and was immediately taken to the Great Khan, the King. The Khan looked at him and asked sternly, "Young spirit, what are you doing here? What are you doing in my Kingdom? Why did you leave your body while it was still alive?"

Stunned, Tarvaa answered, "Great Khan, please forgive me. I thought I was dead! I didn't wait for anyone to summon me or to come and fetch me. I just came to you, and here I am!"

The great Khan was touched by his simplicity and courage. "Young spirit, you must go back to the land of the living. You must return to your body, as your time has not yet come. However, before you leave, I shall grant you a gift from my kingdom: choose whatever your heart desires from my treasures."

Only then did Tarvaa look around him, and in the dimly lit Underworld, he realized that every single pleasure and pain in existence was there: laughter and sadness, wealth and poverty, poetry and dances, good luck and bad luck, and much more. There was also every temptation: those that sometimes bring a sense of happiness and peace and those that often do not. Tarvaa walked amongst the wondrous treasures. He looked left and right but picked none of them. After a long while, something in the shadows caught his eye. He looked closer. This treasure seemed to contain all the other gifts: the tears and the laughter, the songs and the ballads, the dances and even the wisdom of the world. He looked back at the Great Khan, and pointed to the gift. The Khan nodded his approval, impressed by young Tarvaa's choice.

And that, they say, is how the gift of storytelling, with its multitude of stories, legends, and tales, was bestowed upon the spirit of young Tarvaa.

"Now, young spirit, you must return. You must return to your body. Do not come back before we summon you!" said the Khan gravely.

Tarvaa nodded, was taken to the gates, and he undertook the long and dangerous journey back to the land of the living. When he got there, he found his body, but, to his horror, crows had plucked out his eyes from their sockets!

Tarvaa hesitated, distressed. However, he remembered the severe words of the Great Khan, "Do not come back before you are summoned!"

He had no choice: he slipped back into his body.

Against all odds, Tarvaa survived the plague.

Not only did he survive, but he lived to be an old man and throughout his lifetime, he traveled far and wide across Mongolia with its lakes, steppes, vast plains and skies, and its unending mountain ranges. As he walked the land, he told the first stories to come into this world: legends and tales from Mongolia and from distant and exotic places, too. The stories Tarvaa told brought people laughter and tears, dances, ballads and poetry, grief and healing, and, always, wisdom.

And that is how 'Blind Tarvaa'—as he came to be known in Mongolia—the first storyteller of all time and the most talented storyteller of all time, they say, used well the gift bestowed upon him by the Great Khan of the Underworld.

Questions

What gifts have you received from the Underworld/from people who have died/from your ancestors?

Like Tarvaa losing his sight, many people have to live their lives with an enduring loss. Have you had to live with a loss throughout your life? How have you dealt with it?

Sources

There are many written versions of this story on the Internet without the original sources being given. I have written to various people asking for their sources without receiving answers. Before I started telling this story, I sat with a Mongolian lady who gave me a sense of the landscape and people, which is in some ways similar to Ladakh where I spent six months. She also shared some traditional songs on which I base my flute playing when performing this tale. Tarvaa is also mentioned by David Leeming in "The Oxford Companion to World Mythology." However, in that version, he asks for the gift of knowledge from the Khan and subsequently becomes a famous shaman in Mongolia.

Ocean of Tears
A Jewish Story
Retold by Jim Brulé

Once there were two rebbes—Jewish mystics and great teachers—who were great friends. One was known as the Vorker Rebbe, and the other was Menachem Mendel, the Kotzker Rebbe. What surprised people about their great friendship was not that they were both rebbes but that they held such opposing views. The Kotzker Rebbe held exacting standards for truth and accuracy, whereas the Vorker Rebbe was known to be more flexible. This meant that in matters of theology, ethics, and daily living, they would often argue for radically different positions. However, they were so close that when the Vorker Rebbe had his first son, he named him Mendele—a nickname for Mendel, after the Kotzker Rebbe. In fact, it was said that the only love stronger than the love between the Vorker Rebbe and the Kotzker Rebbe was between the Vorker Rebbe and his son.

As was custom, when Mendele grew up to be a man, he became a rebbe as well and moved out to serve a new community. Nevertheless, he and his father wrote to each other daily; a letter would pass in each direction between the two of them. This went on without fail from the day Mendele left home for many, many years.

After so many years, it happened that the Vorker Rebbe died, as happens to us all. Once the period of ritual mourning had passed, Mendele went to the Kotzker Rebbe, for there was a matter that concerned him greatly. "Holy rebbe, I'm concerned. It's been a month, and I haven't received any letters from my father." The fact that Mendele was expecting letters from his father didn't surprise the Kotzker Rebbe; it was well-known that great things were possible for great rebbes, such as the Vorker Rebbe.

The Kotzker Rebbe fell silent, then finally spoke. "You know, I'm also concerned because I used to get letters from your father every day, and I haven't received any either. I'm going to investigate." With this, the Kotzker

Rebbe decided to make a soul ascent and check on the status of his friend.

He knew that after a soul passes on, it ascends in the next world to a height corresponding to the merit achieved in this world. On some occasions, an abode would be prepared for that soul. That merit was often measured by what kind of a student of Torah the person had been; if one were exceptionally meritorious, a person would get a palace there. So, the Kotzker Rebbe began ascending, knowing that his friend was such a good student of Torah that he would probably have to ascend a great deal. After a while, he arrived at the palace of Maimonides.

Maimonides was a great scholar, deeply respected by both Muslims and Jews during his life. The Kotzker Rebbe was so thrilled to be in the palace of Maimonides with all these people gathered around him studying that, at first, he forgot why he was there. Hours passed as he studied with Maimonides—understandably! He thought, *What could be better than this?* As the day ended, he remembered, and went up to Maimonides, saying, "I'm looking for my friend, the Vorker Rebbe. Have you seen him?"

Maimonides smiled at a pleasant memory and replied, "Oh, yes. I've seen him, but he went higher." At that, the Kotzker thanked Maimonides and continued his ascent.

Rising still, the Kotzker finally encountered the palace of Rashi. Even more revered than Maimonides, Rashi was a great commentator on nearly all the scripture ever produced. Once again, the Kotzker was distracted from his quest—naturally! Who would pass over the opportunity to study with Rashi? He studied with Rashi for a week before he remembered his friend. A little embarrassed, he turned to Rashi and asked, "Have you seen my friend, the Vorker Rebbe?"

Rashi smiled broadly, and the Kotzker thought he saw a glimpse of admiration cross his face. "Yes, I have," was the reply. "What an amazing man! His merit was so great—of course, he ascended higher." With that, the Kotzker Rebbe thanked Rashi, took his leave, and ascended higher.

The Kotzker ascended to the palace of Moses—Moses, our teacher! It must have been weeks before he remembered his mission, but once again, Moses directed him higher. *What could be higher? Abraham, our Father!* Could his friend truly have ascended this far?

As he approached Abraham, though, he soon forgot his friend and fell into deep study. When he finally remembered his quest, he became concerned, for he hadn't seen the Vorker at all, and he couldn't imagine what would be higher than Abraham's palace. He meekly approached Abraham, who responded with a puzzling answer, "Oh, yes, he was here, but he didn't stay."

The Kotzker Rebbe's confusion only increased, and he asked, "Can there be any room higher than this? Where could he have gone?"

An entirely new look passed over Abraham's face. Was it admiration or something different—pity? Amazement? "Oh," he said. "He didn't go higher."

"Not higher? Well, then, where can I find him?"

Avraham Avinu, Abraham our Father, paused. "You'll have to descend." There was another pause as the Kotzker Rebbe's confusion grew. "You'll have to descend to the center of the deepest, darkest forest on earth."

Not knowing what else to do, the Kotzker Rebbe began his descent, and the speed was like a star falling from the sky. It was not hard to find the darkest forest, like a dark shadow on the face of the earth. As he made his way toward the center of it, the darkness grew so great that he couldn't fly anymore; he had to walk.

With each step, it became more difficult to move until, finally, off in the distance, the darkness seemed to lighten. It wasn't quite as dark, but the sounds coming from that place took the Kotzker Rebbe's breath away!

At first, it sounded like people sighing, but as he got closer, the sighs seemed to become moans. As he grew closer still, they became wails; a rhythmic wailing, over and over, sounding directly into his heart. When he finally stepped further into that space, he saw a great ocean before him—an ocean with waves that crashed. Now, the Kotzker saw the source of the sound. As every wave crashed, he heard the wails.

He could barely move, but he looked down the beach, and there he saw his friend. The Kotzker Rebbe gathered his strength and ran over to him, saying, "What are you doing here? What is this place? Why are you here?"

The Vorker Rebbe noticed him for the first time and turned slowly to face him, silent.

As he drew closer, the Kotzker Rebbe cried again, "Yitzhak, my friend, what is this place?"

Pain raced across the Vorker Rebbe's face as he croaked out an answer, "This is the Ocean of Tears."

Finally reaching him, the Kotzker Rebbe's heart, already wounded by the wailing, started to break again—his friend was filled with so much pain. "The Ocean of Tears? What is that? And why are you here?"

A new fire came over the Vorker's whole being. His voice strengthened as he began, "These are the tears that are cried by all those in pain."

He paused and then passionately raised his fist to the sky, crying, "And I told the Holy One that I would not ascend any further until He dried up all these tears!"

Questions
What can we learn from the values of those who have departed? What do we want others to know is more important than fame to us?

Sources
I first heard this story told by Maggid Daniel Lev, a *hassid* of Rabbi Shlomo Carlebach. It is found in Schwartz, Howard, "Leaves from the Garden of Eden," who also collected it from Rabbi Carlebach. Schwartz notes that a variant of it appears in *Sippurei Hasidim*, edited by Shlomo Yosef Zevin (Tel Aviv, 1964).

The River Olu
A Yoruba Story
Retold by Jim Brulé

Many years ago in Yorubaland, there was a terrible famine. It was more severe than anyone could remember. There was no rain for weeks, the crops all withered, and even the animals fled. A hunter and his wife decided to flee with their children—a daughter and a son—in search of a land where they could survive.

Their journey led them across dry fields and down dusty paths. They carried their scant food and water on their backs. They hoped that they would find something along the way, but there was nothing—no food and no water. Finally, one day, they saw a forest on the horizon. Filled with hope, the father lifted his spear and said to his wife, "Wait here; wait with the children. I shouldn't be long." He shouldered his spear and loped off to the distant trees while the mother and their children waited, filled with anticipation. They waited for hours, until sunset, and then all through the night. They waited from morning and midday to another sunset, but the father did not come back.

"We are hungry, Mother," whimpered the children plaintively. "We are so hungry, and we are thirsty. We are hungry, thirsty, and so tired. We are hungry, Mother!" Her heart broke as she sang softly to her children, singing a song of comfort and hope. Finally, they fell asleep in her lap, and the stars appeared in the night sky.

The next morning, her husband had not returned. The two children still lay in her lap, barely moving. She tore her dress and covered their faces with the scrap. She said, "Children, you wait here—wait for me. I shall go. I will find us food or water, but hopefully both." She lifted her calabash onto her back and went to search. Hour after hour passed, and she found nothing. When evening came, she returned to her children, who were now even weaker than before.

"We are thirsty, Mother, so very thirsty, Mother! Water...we need water!" Her heart broke again; she had found none. She looked into the empty calabash she was holding. Not a drop of moisture was to be found. In desperation, she went back into the forest, searching for water. She didn't need a river, she didn't even need a pond—just a puddle would do! But there was nothing—the drought dried everything to the bone. She cried in anguish, but she couldn't even shed tears. So, she returned to her children with nothing.

She felt she would explode in agony. Shaking her fist to the cloudless sky, she cried out, "I cannot! I cannot see my children die. I cannot! I would rather die." Then, she heard their whispers, so very faint and dry. "We are dying, Mother," they said. "We are dying, Mother! Help us, Mother... we are dying."

Her heart shattered—she could not bear to see those she gave birth to die. She looked at the empty calabash that she held in her hands. She lifted it over her head, shook it to the sky, and then smashed it at her feet. Empty, dry, it shattered—like her hopes, empty and broken.

In that moment, however, she felt an unexpected power rising in her—the visceral drive to care for her children, to prevent their suffering and demise. Suddenly, in an instant, she turned into a river—the River Olu—and flowed over her children. They opened their mouths and drank deeply from the river that had been their mother. Soon, they felt life returning to their bodies, filling their beings. They drank and were refreshed and nourished, and they survived until the famine was over.

The descendants of that mother and her children are called the Children of the River Olu, the river that flows in the Odogbolu kingdom of Yoruba land. It is known that whenever they drink or bathe in the river, their thirst will be quenched, and their illnesses healed. Whenever the Children of the River Olu drink the water from the River or bathe in its currents, they become strong.

Even more significantly, should a Child of the River Olu have, as their very first drink, the water of the River Olu, it brings a special power: they can only speak the truth. With this power comes a special burden, for whatever they say of someone, be it good or ill, it will be true. And so the Children of the River Olu are taught to only speak well of others, so that the world may be filled will good.

Question
In what ways do our ancestors bless us beyond whatever failures they may have encountered?

Sources
There are two versions of this story from the same people. One version is the first I heard, told by Titi Ogunnaike, a Yoruba storyteller, who told this story as it had been passed down to her. In this version, the mother is the one transformed into the River Olu. A second version is told by the Priest of the River Olu, in which it is the father who is transformed. I have heard this second version in a video recording by Ms. Ogunnaike at an event we organized to record the telling by the King of Odogbolu and the Priest of the River.

Told by Titi Ogunnaike: https://vimeo.com/841540908
Told by the Priest: https://www.youtube.com/watch?v=GJSVIyIA8Oc

The Tear Jar
A Jewish Story from Syria
Retold by Jim Brulé

The drought lasted for a very long time: the grasses were dry, the earth was hard, the streams were empty, and the crops were dying. The community came to the rabbi. Their spokesman, Yitzhak, said, "Rabbi, you must help us. This drought seems endless. What can we do?" The rabbi replied, "We must all pray; each of us must pray. Go to your homes and pray with all your souls."

So, each person went to their home, and they prayed for hours. The next day, there wasn't a cloud in the sky. They went back to the rabbi and demanded something more powerful. The rabbi thought and considered and said, "Everyone must fast for a day and then pray for a day." Each person went home and fasted and prayed, and the sun beat down on them even more, with even more heat than before.

When the rain failed to come, they returned to the rabbi. "Rabbi, we're dying! We need water. What must we do?" The rabbi went into his office. They could hear him turning the pages of books, unrolling and rolling ancient scrolls. Finally, he emerged, saying, "We must have an even more powerful prayer. For this, we must gather as a community—one people in one place, fasting and praying together. And we must begin right away—at sundown!"

The word went out, and soon the synagogue was full. To be sure that everyone was present, the *shammash*—the caretaker of the synagogue—started counting people, and a frown crossed his face. He whispered to the rabbi, "We're missing someone."

The rabbi raised his voice to everyone and said, "Look around! Who is not here? Who are we missing? We need everyone here!"

After a pause and rumblings of confused voices, someone called out, "I know. It's Chava, the widow! She lives outside the town; nobody's seen her for such a long time."

Of course, the rabbi thought, filled with remorse. *The widow Chava.* The community had merely tolerated her merchant husband; his prices always seemed to rise when people had the greatest need, but he always had what was needed. At his urging, the community fed her through the first week of mourning, but then...everyone forgot. *How many years ago had that been?*

The rabbi immediately sent the *shammash* out to fetch her while the congregation waited. Every moment was agony as they waited and waited for the doors of the synagogue to open. Finally, in walked old Chava, carrying a jar. Her clothes were simple and worn, but clean. She walked up slowly to the rabbi, then turned to the community, surveying those present, each of whom lowered their eyes when they met. Finally, she spoke, her words spilling pain.

"You want me here? You want me here now? You want me to help you? After you abandoned me all these years? You want me to help you when you abandoned me after my husband died? You left me on my own. Now, you want me to help you get rain? For all those years, I did not feel your tears, only my own."

She held up the jar, showing it to everyone, "This is my jar of tears. These are all the tears I have cried—on my own. I collected them as my only true possessions. They are all I have of my husband, my losses, and my sorrows. Since your God will not bring you rain, perhaps I should smash this jar of tears on the floor, for that will be the only rain you get."

At that very moment, thunder was heard, and soon, rain began to fall in a great torrent. The people got up and cheered and danced in great relief. Amidst their rejoicing, singing, and dancing, no one saw Chava leave. They danced and rejoiced all night.

The next morning, when the people were leaving the synagogue, they saw a tree that had not been there the day before. Only the *shammash* knew that it was growing in the place where Chava had poured her tears out on the ground. There, in that spot, grew a pomegranate tree, whose fruit resembles tears. More tears than the year has days; as many tears as the Law has commandments.

Questions
How do we release our pent-up grief and put it to good use? How do we approach those who are overcome with grief?

Sources
This story can be found in many places; I encountered it in Ellen Frankel's *The Classic Tales* and Peninnah Schram's *Stories Within Stories*. Another excellent retelling is in Raphael Patai's *Gates to the Old City*. It has been told by Jewish communities in Syria and Yemen.

(Im)mortality

(IM)MORTALITY

The Camel Driver
A Muslim Story
Retold by Jim Brulé

Ahmed, the merchant, was successful by anyone's measure; his customers extended over many miles. He traveled from city to city, from marketplace to marketplace, buying and selling his items. Ahmed loved the variety of people and places he encountered.

Ahmed, like most, transported his merchandise across the desert by caravan—in his case, over 700 camels, with just a handful of drivers. This would be a huge challenge without a good lead camel, especially since camels can be rather irascible. Ahmed had a favorite camel to lead the train: it had a calm personality, seemed to know just what Ahmed wanted, and would convey what was expected to the other camels in a way that only camels knew. This camel was in the lead whenever they set out, and the hundreds of others would fall in line at the right moment. Over time, a tremendous bond was forged between Ahmed and this camel.

One day, while traveling to a larger city, they came across an orchard of pomegranates. Dark, red fruit hung from every branch; the orchard was surrounded by only the most nominal of fences. In fact, one of the branches was dangling over the edge of the fence, weighed down by a particularly large pomegranate. When Ahmed's favorite camel saw this pomegranate, it reached up, opened its massive mouth—seemingly unhinging its jaw—and snapped that pomegranate up in a single bite. A river of red juice flowed down its chin as it crunched through the hard, thick skin, and the camel almost smiled at tasting that big, sweet, bitter flavor.

Now, unbeknownst to anyone, the orchard's owner happened to be nearby, just inside the fence. When he saw the camel reach up and bite one of his fresh pomegranates, he became angry. He yelled at it to get away, but the camel just smiled, munching. "Get away!" he yelled. Then he picked up a stone and threw it. The stone hit the camel right between the eyes, and it collapsed. Ahmed ran over to it, kneeled down, and cried out—it was dead!

Ahmed was enraged. His favorite camel—his most worthy camel—had been killed for eating a pomegranate! His ears rang, and his pulse pounded. He reached down, picked up the rock, and, screaming, hurled it back at the orchard owner. As fate would have it, the rock struck the owner between the eyes, knocking him to the ground.

Everything was suddenly silent.

Unknown to Ahmed or the other camel drivers, the sons of the orchard owner had heard the commotion and were running over to see what was going on. When they saw their father fall to the ground, they raced over to him to revive him.

But he was dead.

They erupted and raced to Ahmed, screaming furiously. They began pummeling him, crying, "You've killed our father, you've killed our father. You'll pay with your life!"

Ahmed's camel drivers jumped into the fray, trying to pull the sons off Ahmed, but soon it descended into a brawl. Fortunately, some of the Sultan's guards happened to be traveling along the same road and came upon the scene. They separated everyone and then demanded an explanation.

The eldest brother screamed that Ahmed killed their father and that Ahmed must pay with his life. At that, Ahmed fell to his knees and acknowledged that he threw the rock that killed their father. He swore it was an accident, explaining that he lost his temper when the owner killed his precious camel. He then offered to make the standard blood payment for the father's death for the terrible loss of life.

The brothers refused. Ahmed pleaded. They went back and forth, over and over, until it seemed that another brawl would erupt. So, the head of the guards bound Ahmed and headed off to the Sultan's palace, with the brothers close behind—furious, demanding his life.

There was such a commotion as they entered the grand courtyard that the Sultan looked out of his room to try to make sense of it all. He summoned the captain of the guards, who described what happened. The Sultan nodded and told him to gather everyone in the courtyard, and he would hear the case. The Sultan stepped into the courtyard a few minutes later, and the trial began. A crowd had already started to gather.

First, the eldest son spoke and described how Ahmed, the camel merchant, killed their father; he and his brothers demanded his life in payment. Then, Ahmed recalled how he lost his beloved camel because their father threw a stone and that he'd lost his temper. He explained that he did not intend to kill the man and that he was willing to pay the blood price. The Sultan listened and asked a small question here and a small question there. The crowd continued to grow.

Finally, he drew over the elder son and said, "Listen, my son. The terrible facts are clear. You have the right to demand a life for life. But you also have the right to accept the blood payment; it's your decision. I urge you to let the killing stop here and to accept the blood payment." Not even a moment passed before the son announced his decision, "I demand his life—there is no amount of gold that will replace my father!"

The Sultan looked wearily upon him. Sighing, he said, "That is our law; that is your choice, so it shall be."

The Sultan summoned the executioner, who brought his blood-stained block and gleaming sword. He set the block down before Ahmed, who knelt over it with his hands bound behind his back. Ahmed laid his head against the block, his neck fitting into the stained groove. The executioner lifted his sword, and a hush fell on the crowd. Before it could come down, Ahmed lifted his head and called out to the Sultan, "Your Majesty! Is it not true that the condemned man gets a final request?"

"Yes, it is so. Go ahead, make your final request."

"Your Majesty, I have a family who lives a day from here. I have accounts that must be settled to preserve their name. For if I die without them being settled, my family will be called thieves. I beg you, your Majesty, give me three days: one day to travel to my family, the second to say my goodbyes and settle my accounts. And on the third day, I promise, I will return and pay the price with my life."

The brother was outraged, and the Sultan laughed loudly, "Do you expect me to think you'll return if I let you go? What kind of fool do you take me for? I cannot grant such a request. Kneel and receive your punishment."

The crowd murmured and then fell silent. The executioner lifted his sword a second time. Suddenly, a single voice emerged from the crowd, "Wait! Oh, majestic Sultan, wait! I have a solution." The Sultan looked at the speaker, confused and intrigued. "I will stand as hostage for this man. Take me and hold me for those three days. If, on the third day, he has not returned, you may have my life in his stead."

The Sultan was stunned, "Do you realize what you're offering? Do you know this man has no reason to return? Do you know that your life will almost certainly be forfeit?" The speaker nodded, understanding.

"I have never heard such a thing!" the Sultan exclaimed to himself, but he thought about it, considered it, and realized it fell within the rules. He raised his hand and authorized the bargain. The hostage was bound and led off to a cell.

The Sultan spoke sternly to Ahmed, "Three days!" With that, Ahmed leaped onto the swiftest horse he could find and rode off through the gates and into the desert.

The three days passed quickly; no one expected Ahmed to return early, but many expected him to return. So when the evening of the third day began to fall, and there was no Ahmed, his supporters wondered. Even the Sultan hoped that Ahmed would return, so as the hours stretched on and there was no Ahmed, the Sultan grew more unhappy.

The sun set, and the eldest son demanded payment. The Sultan urged patience—to wait until morning. The son fumed and stood in the courtyard, arms crossed. The crowd began returning as the night lost its darkness and morning began to arrive. As the sun rose without Ahmed, the Sultan reluctantly summoned the guards to bring the hostage from the cell. The executioner placed the block in the center of the courtyard; the crowd grew to its fullest, and the hostage knelt before the block.

As he laid his head on the block, the hostage looked up to the executioner and said, "Please make it swift!" The executioner, with perhaps the slightest expression of commiseration, nodded. He drew his sword to prepare for the final blow; silence fell. Suddenly, someone called out, "Look! Dust! Maybe it's Ahmed!"

The Sultan held up his hand for a pause, and everyone rushed to look. As the dust grew closer and closer, a person could be seen on a horse riding at great speed. Soon, they could tell that it was indeed Ahmed. He came racing in through the gates, leaped off the horse, and called out to the executioner, "Wait! I'm here, I'm here!"

Ahmed raced to the Sultan and fell on his knees, thanking him for waiting. He explained that he had come as quickly as he could but was delayed by a sandstorm. With that, he walked over to the executioner's block and lifted the hostage, who was quickly unbound. Then Ahmed knelt at the block and laid his head once again across the bloody groove.

A guard bound the hands of Ahmed behind him, muttering to himself, "Why did you return?" The executioner drew his sword, and Ahmed whispered to him, "Please, make it swift." Again, the executioner nodded slightly, then raised his sword, gleaming in the sunlight. Suddenly, the Sultan called, "Wait! Ahmed, why did you return?" The executioner rested his sword as Ahmed lifted his head to respond.

"Your Majesty, the thought of whether I should return certainly came to me over and over. But I asked myself, 'What kind of world do I want to live in? Do I want to live in a world where a person's word means something or not?' And the answer was simple—this is the world I choose to live in. And so, I had to return."

The Sultan nodded, understanding. The executioner drew another breath and raised his sword again, high in the sky.

But the Sultan called out, "Wait! I also have a choice. I also have to ask myself, 'What kind of world do I want to live in?' My answer is that I want to live in a world in which justice and mercy both thrive. So," he turned to the executioner, "put down your sword and release this man." Then he turned to the eldest son.

"You will accept the blood price. Now let the three of us—Ahmed, you, and I—go and share some tea."

And with that, they retired from the courtyard—together.

Questions
What values are important to you in this world? When you have to make a difficult choice, what guides you?

Sources
The story is attributed to an unspecified hadith. I first heard this story told by Jan Blake on TEDxTalks, 2011 https://youtu.be/czcWfM2KHFk

The Master of the Garden
An Armenian Story
Retold by Rebecca Claire Lemaire

Once, there was an Armenian King whose palace was surrounded by the most magnificent gardens, tended by the very best gardeners of the land. The great variety of trees, flowers, and plants all bloomed beautifully in the spring and summer, and some flowers even bloomed in the winter.

Amongst the plants, there was a little rose tree; it was sickly, thin, and scrawny—a single stalk that carried a couple of dried-up branches and a few brownish leaves. For as long as anyone could remember, it had never given any flowers, and yet, this rose tree was very special to the King. It even had its own gardener, whose sole job was to look after it. This rose tree was the Anahakan rose tree. Not only was it very rare, but it was also mentioned in the old scriptures: *One day, the Anahakan rose tree will give the purest and most beautiful of flowers, which will bestow Immortality upon the Master of the garden.*

Immortality...eternal youth, pondered the King dreamily, imagining the Anahakan in full bloom. Every morning, the King would jump out of bed, get dressed, run into the gardens, and inspect the Anahakan to see if there was any change, any sign of a flower to come. He would then turn to his gardener, "Remember," he would say impatiently, "You have until the end of summer! If no flower has bloomed, your head will roll!"

But spring came and went, then summer came and went. There were still no flowers on the Anahakan. The gardener was replaced....

Twelve years passed, and...twelve gardeners passed. The King felt irritated and depressed and wondered where else he could look for a capable gardener.

One morning, as the King was grumbling and complaining to his Prime

Minister about the lack of flowers on the Anahakan and the useless gardeners of his land, a very young man called Samvel presented himself at the palace and asked the King for the opportunity to take care of the Anahakan rose tree.

The King laughed sarcastically, "You are just a boy! Look at you, inexperienced and young, thinking you can succeed where the best and most experienced gardeners have failed!"

Samvel stayed silent.

The King looked into Samvel's dark eyes and asked, "You know the price for failure, don't you?"

"I do," said Samvel.

"And you dare?"

"I do."

The King had nothing to lose. *I'll use him while I look for another experienced gardener,* he thought. He led Samvel to the rose tree, "You have until the end of next summer," he said. Then, he went back to the affairs of the palace.

Samvel tended the Anahakan rose tree: he pruned it, fed it, cleaned the soil around its roots, and did all that the other gardeners had done...and more:

Day and night,
Samvel sat by the Anahakan
Watched over the Anahakan
Sang lullabies to the Anahakan
Whispered poetry to the Anahakan
Repeated the name of the Anahakan
And, sometimes, he danced for the Anahakan

The King no longer jumped out of bed every morning to come and see the

Anahakan rose tree, and Samvel hardly ever saw him.

When winter came with its terrible winds, storms, and rain, Samvel sheltered the Anahakan with his own body and continued whispering to the rose tree. At the beginning of springtime, the flowers of the gardens began to bloom—one after the other—healthy, colorful, and fragrant, but Samvel still only had eyes for the Anahakan rose tree:

Day and night,
Samvel sat by the Anahakan
Watched over the Anahakan
Sang lullabies to the Anahakan
Whispered poetry to the Anahakan
Repeated the name of the Anahakan
And, sometimes, he danced for the Anahakan

Throughout the spring months, Samvel continued to tend the Anahakan, caring for it and watching over it. At times, though, he despaired. *Is it worth it?*, he wondered.

However, when summer spread its warmth over the gardens, Samvel was still there, sitting, watching, singing, whispering, chanting, and dancing.

One day, in the midst of the summer heat, he looked at the Anahakan rose tree and asked in a broken voice, "Where is your pain, Anahakan? What is your pain?"

He'd barely finished his question when a big, slimy, black worm crawled out from the roots of the Anahakan rose tree.

As Samvel bent down to pick it up and have a look at it, a swallow flew down, landed on his hand, picked up the worm in its beak, and flew back up into the sky!

When Samvel looked back down at the Anahakan, he immediately knew something was different. During the next few days, he continued to observe, and he watched as slowly—ever so slowly—the Anahakan rose tree was infused with a new life. Its leaves turned greener, and its stalk and branches grew stronger as if the sap was flowing more freely.

Day and night,
Samvel sat by the Anahakan
Watched over the Anahakan
Sang lullabies to the Anahakan
Whispered poetry to the Anahakan
Repeated the name of the Anahakan
And, sometimes, he danced for the Anahakan

Suddenly, one day, towards the end of the summer, a tiny, very tiny bud appeared on one of the branches. Samvel caressed it, sang lullabies, and whispered poetry to the bud. During the next few days, he watched as it grew bigger and as it slowly opened and turned into the most beautiful of roses.

He asked somebody to fetch the King, and very soon, the shouts and cries and laughter of the King were heard throughout the gardens. "Is it true? Is it true it has flowered? Is there a rose? Am I truly immortal? Oh! Eternal youth for me!"

When he reached the rose tree and saw it was true, the King laughed and hugged Samvel, "I always knew you could do it! I will bury you in gold!"

And after reflection, he said gravely, "But you, young man, cannot leave now...nor ever. You shall continue to take care of this rose tree until the day you die!"

"I shall," answered Samvel, smiling.

A hut was built for Samvel so he'd be more comfortable. A fence was placed around the rose tree, and the King declared that only Samvel was allowed to go near the Anahakan. Banquets and concerts were organized in the palace to celebrate the King's immortality and eternal youth while Samvel continued doing what he had done all along:

Day and night,
Samvel sat by the Anahakan
Watched over the Anahakan
Sang lullabies to the Anahakan
Whispered poetry to the Anahakan
Repeated the name of the Anahakan
And, sometimes, he danced for the Anahakan

The days passed, then weeks, months, and years.

Ten years later, the King fell gravely ill. Although the best doctors in the land were called to find a cure for the King's failing body, they all agreed nothing could be done.

One evening, the King called Samvel to his bedside. "It was all a lie," the King said weakly, "the Master of the garden is going to die, just like everyone else."

Samvel quietly gasped. He realized, *The Master of the garden! It was never the King...I...I....*

His eyes widened in awe, and he stood there, his mouth slightly open....

He was aware of an indescribable, timeless expansion that was familiar and surprising all at once....

There was a long, peaceful silence, and in that pure stillness, maybe the King had a glimpse of the Essence of his Being too.....

The King let out his last breath. Samvel gently closed his eyes and kissed his forehead.

He sat by the King's side for a long while; he sang, he whispered poetry, he chanted, and he rested in vibrant Silence.

When Samvel finally stepped out into the gardens, it was nighttime. He looked up, "Good night," he said to one of the stars in the sky. "Good night," he said to another. "Good night...good night...good night..." You see, now, he had all the time in the world—he had Eternity.

Question
What does the rose represent for you?

Imagine that the rose is the core of your Being–the Heart–write a poem or lullaby to the rose.

Sources
I first read this story in a book called "Les Questions des Petits sur la Mort" written by Marie Aubinais, published in 2010. I also found different versions on the Internet, usually in French (in les Contes du Louvre, for example, retold by Constance Félix). I then found this story in Gougaud's book "L' Arbre d'Amour et de Sagesse."

I sat with an Armenian lady to talk about the story and get a feel for the culture, language, and music. The name Samvel means 'Godly', and the music I play on the flute when performing this story is based on a piece of music I heard played on the *duduk*. It is called *Akh Maral Djan*, roughly translated as 'Oh! My dear Maral' (Maral being a girl/woman's name).

(IM)MORTALITY

The Reincarnated Maggid
A Jewish Story
Retold by Jim Brulé

A *maggid* is the least known type of Jewish clergy, ordained to lift people spiritually through stories. The *maggidim* (pl) are itinerants; they move from place to place, whereas the other clergy—rabbi and cantor—are attached to a congregation and don't circulate around.

There once was a *maggid* who was very well-traveled, very well-known, and very much beloved. He spent his life traveling from place to place, lifting people up spiritually with his stories—he knew he was reaching their souls. In this way, through all these encounters, he deepened his own wisdom and his love for the people he encountered grew and grew. Whenever he would come to a village, he would go to the local Jewish community and announce his presence. They would gather for an afternoon or an evening, or maybe even a full day of stories. They would feed him, give him a place to stay, and then he would move on to the next place. This was his life, and he was very fulfilled.

As he grew older and older, it came to him that he would only be telling stories a little while longer. It happened that among the amazing stories he acquired, there was one story that he had yet to tell because it was so rich, and so deep, and so long. The *maggid* wanted to be sure to tell this story before he died. So he returned to his home village, where he was much beloved. He approached the rabbi and said, "I have a need to tell this story; a big, long story. Please, would you arrange for me to do that?"

There was no question that the rabbi would help. He enlisted all the leaders of the community who rented a huge hall because they knew many people would want to come. They ensured there were enough rooms in inns and homes because they knew this would take quite a long time—days, perhaps even weeks! Finally, the appointed day came.

The hall they set aside was quite large. There was a balcony all around, and the rafters were high above that. In the center was a small fire, and torches were hung all around the walls. People streamed in from everywhere, excited to hear the story. Finally, the *maggid* walked in, and a hush descended. He did not, however, begin immediately; he waited until the room was completely full. Finally, he stepped to the center and drew his first breath. The people were rapt in their attention; they listened with their whole hearts.

The story went on for hour after hour. Soon after it began, angels assembled in the rafters—they wanted to hear this story as well. The *maggid's* voice rose and fell; he sang, and he whispered; he moved and stood still, and everyone was transfixed. Hours passed, then two days, and then three days. No one even thought about how the story would end because everyone was so enraptured. They couldn't even conceive of it ending!

Suddenly, unseen by anyone, the Angel of Death arrived. Swiftly, in mid-sentence, he reached down and took the *maggid's* soul. Just like that, the story stopped. The Angel of Death departed so swiftly he didn't even hear the crowd gasp.

Instead, the Angel of Death took the *maggid* up to his palace and said, "Good! Now, your story is mine. Tell me the rest of the story. I want this story." The *maggid* merely glared at him, not speaking a word. The Angel of Death smiled a crooked smile, understanding the *maggid's* refusal but also knowing that he always got his way. So he spoke again to the *maggid*, "No, no, you don't understand: you're mine now. I'm the only one you can tell the story to. You must tell me the story." The *maggid* remained silent. Finally, the Angel of Death said, "You may not appreciate how patient a being I can be. If you won't tell me the story, then it will never be told. This is where you're going to stay."

No one knows how to measure time in the next world, but the silence continued for a long time. Every now and then, the Angel of Death would try to cajole the *maggid* into finishing the story. Every time, the *maggid* would just stay silent. It was in this way that the stalemate continued.

The other angels also wanted to hear the end of the story, and they knew that the Angel of Death was holding the *maggid*. So they came to the Angel of Death and asked him to compromise. The Angel of Death thought about it. Finally, he went to the *maggid* and said, "I understand you don't want to tell me the story. However, the rest of the angels have petitioned me. They would love to hear the story. So, let us compromise—you can tell them the end of the story, and I will listen in. Agreed?"

At that, the *maggid* spoke, "Angels don't need stories—people do." Then he returned to his silence. Despite all the waiting and cajoling, it was clear that the *maggid* would not tell the story.

Finally, the Angel of Death succumbed, "I'll let you be reborn as long as you tell the story." The *maggid* nodded his agreement, but there was a problem—the angel Lailah. It is well understood that when a soul is waiting to be born, it knows everything: everything that has happened and will happen. However, when the child is born, the angel Lailah comes down and taps the baby on the upper lip so they forget everything. They have to start learning all over again. This was the problem—the *maggid* would forget his story when he was born!

So, the Angel of Death went to Lailah to ask for an exception. Here, no cajoling was necessary—she wanted to hear the story, too. The deal was made.

Shortly thereafter, a young girl was born. As her mother lifted her to her breast, the young girl spoke—the infant, just born, spoke! She said, "Mother, I have a story to tell." Thankfully, her mother didn't drop her. Instead, she cried out to her husband, who came running in. "Our baby is talking to me! Our baby is talking to me!"

"Yes, yes..." he began, knowing this to be impossible but not wanting to argue with his wife.

"No, listen—she's talking!"

At that moment, the baby spoke up and said, "Father, I have a story to tell..."

Both parents were speechless. "Please," she said. "You must help me..." Then, the baby girl described all that happened. The father ran to the rabbi and asked her to gather all the people she could because the story must be told to as many people as possible. Soon, people began to assemble, the parents took their child out on the porch, and many, many people gathered in circles. It was likely that much of the crowd just wanted to see a speaking infant who was less than a day old, story or not. Above, the angels came as well—even the Angel of Death. Soon, the young *maggidah* began to tell her story, which went on for hours and hours and days and days. When she finally finished, the angel Lailah came and tapped on her lip, and she immediately began to cry. Her mother took her to her breast, and her next life began.

Question
What kind of stories do you hope will be told about you?

Source
This story is retold by Howard Schwartz as *The Angel's Gift* in "Invisible Kingdoms," Harpercollins, 2002. He reports that this is based on Israel Folk Archives story 4591, a Polish story, and Israel Folk Archives story 14728, a Moroccan story.

The Siddha and the Jnani
An Indian Story
Retold by Rebecca Claire Lemaire

Some traditional forms of yoga in India place a focus on experientially studying the different elements in nature. Through exercises and practices, yogis learn to control the mind and the way the elements move through the body-mind system, which may lead to *'siddhis'*. The word *'siddhi,'* from Sanskrit, can roughly be translated as 'miraculous or occult powers imparted by the late stages of intense discipline and meditation.' The yogi who has reached *'siddhis'* is called a *'siddha.'* It is not unusual to hear stories about yogis who have lived more than three hundred years, yogis who have been seen flying across the Himalayan skies, or who can, through manipulation of the elements, disintegrate and manifest in another time and place.

The word 'yoga' is often translated as yoke or union.

This story is about Allama Prabhulinga or Allama Prabhu, a 'Jnana Yogi' or 'Jnani' (yogi of knowledge, yogi of wisdom), a great sage from North Karnataka in the 12th century who is also famous for his mystical poetry.

Allama Prabhubinga was sometimes called 'Ocean of Grace,' 'The Conqueror of Illusion,' or even 'Incarnate Void and Spaciousness.' One day, he was wandering the mountains of Western India alone—as he often did—when he arrived at a little hut, the dwellings of a yogi called Gorakkar. Gorakkar was a very powerful *siddha* yogi who, through lifetimes of discipline and yoga techniques, had managed to turn his body into what they call a *vajrakaya*—a diamond body, unconquerable and resistant like a diamond. This meant that he had freed himself from old age, freed himself from illness; freed himself from...death. He was said to be over two hundred years old at the time of this story.

When Gorakkar saw the sage, Allama Prabhulinga, coming toward his hut, he immediately knew that he was a powerful yogi, too. *An equal*, he thought. Consequently, he did not prostrate as people did when they met

Allama. Gorakkar greeted him standing up, and said, "Welcome, stranger. Who are you?"

Allama, knowing perfectly well what he was doing, answered, "Only the one who has gotten rid of the ego illusion would understand Who I am." Gorakkar's eyes opened wide, then, smirking, "Do you know who *I* am? I am a *vajrakaya* yogi who has conquered death! How dare you talk to me like that?"

Allama did not answer, but, smiling, looked deeply into the eyes of Gorakkar who thought he saw, in the sage's peaceful smiling gaze, a shade of disdain. Outraged, Gorakkar picked up a long, sharp sword and gave it to Allama.

"Strike me!" he said. "Go on! Try to cut me in half! If just one piece of my skin is hurt, then I'm not a *siddha* yogi, and I will prostrate before you."

Knowing perfectly well what he was doing, Allama took the sword and struck hard. The sword bounced off Gorakkar's head; there was a great thunderous noise, the neighboring wild animals and flocks of birds fled in panic, and there was a sudden downpour of rain.

Allama smiled, "Well done!" he said. "You've made a very powerful sound with your body and made it rain. But my dear Gorakkar, I shall tell you a secret: whatever has a beginning also has an end. You've only lengthened the life span of your body—possibly by many hundreds of years—but it *will* die, because, one day, it was born."

He continued, smiling, "It doesn't matter whether your body is immortal or not, because You are not your body. Investigate Who you truly are."

Gorakkar was not listening. "Did you not see what just happened?" he interrupted Allama. "What would happen if I struck *you* with a sword? Tell me!" Gorakkar picked up the sword, "Let me strike you, and we shall see what will happen to you!"

Allama, silent, waited. Gorakkar hesitated; he didn't want to kill anyone.

However, once again, he thought he saw disdain in the eyes of the sage, who said, "Strike!" with such calm authority that Gorakkar saw red and struck him hard.

What happened next almost made Gorakkar lose his balance. The sword passed through Allama's body as though it was cutting through...nothing at all; as if it was sweeping through a ray of light. Gorakkar, astonished, swept the sword left and right and up and down through Allama's spaciousness.

"*You?* You are the Supreme Light I worship?" Gorakkar asked in awe. He fell to his knees and prostrated at Allama's feet, asking him to be his *guru*; his master and guide. That is how Gorakkar came to be one of Allama's closest disciples and abandoned everything that was not the Absolute Truth. Under Allama's guidance, he investigated the Spaciousness of his Being as capacity for the world; that which he truly was...is—neither this nor that, but rather 'That which is All' or 'That which is not.'

And that is how Gorakkar learned that only by acknowledging his true Self—the Heart of his being—could he truly be freed from death. Eventually, ideas of death and immortality disappeared completely from his consciousness.

Only the Light of his Being remained.

Question

What is the Light of your Being? Put your timer on for 7 minutes and write a stream of consciousness starting with, "The Light of my Being is...."

Sources

I first read this story as *The Jnani and The Siddha* in "Spiritual Stories as told by Ramana Maharshi," Sri Ramanasramam, Tiruvannamalai Fifth edition 1999.

There are more written and oral versions on the Internet (e.g. David Godman) as well as in the book "Crumbs from his Table" by Ramanananda Swarnagiri, also published by Ramanashram Tiruvanamalai.

The original version appears in the *Prabhulinga Leelai*, a 15th-century Virasaiva work written in Kannada by a Virasaiva scholar, Camarasa, and comprising 1,111 verses. It was then translated into Tamil verse by Sivaprakasa Swamigal, an accomplished Virasaiva poet and scholar, in the seventeenth century. The Tamil version was read by Ramana Maharshi, who referred to it in his conversations with visitors on several occasions.

Note: According to David Godman, while the stories published by Ramanashram mention the *siddha* yogi as Goraknath, it seems that Goraknath was a famous north Indian yogi who lived between the sixth and ninth centuries, while Gorakkar is a different man, a yogi in the 12th century who strived hard to extend his lifespan and to make his body impervious to harm.

Biographies

Jim Brulé is a multifaceted individual whose life's work revolves around transformational storytelling, spiritual exploration, and end-of-life care. With advanced degrees in counseling psychology and artificial intelligence, Jim's journey is a blend of intellectual pursuit and heartfelt service. His ordination as a spiritual storyteller in the Jewish tradition—a *maggid*—laid the foundation for his online school, Transformational Storytelling, which since 2016 has been nurturing spiritual storytellers from around the globe, and is accredited by the National Storytelling Network.

As a death doula, Jim provides compassionate guidance to individuals and families navigating the end of life, a calling fortified by his Master's in Counseling Psychology and certifications from the National End-of-Life Doula Alliance (NEDA) and The Dying Year. His service extends to various hospice centers, an Omega home for the dying, and as an on-call chaplain specializing in end-of-life and trauma care at large university hospitals.

Jim's online programs such as "Journey through Dying and Living" and "Legacy Storytelling," offer a beacon of support to those grappling with mortality and legacy. His storytelling series, including "Stories for Healing" and "Diving Deeply into Stories," have reached a global audience, exploring multicultural narratives and end-of-life themes.

His initiative "Welcoming the Other" employs storytelling to foster empathy and understanding towards the 'other,' encouraging communities to bridge divides of faith, ethnicity, privilege, and class. Jim's storytelling also extends to interfaith study groups, exploring the close comparison of Jewish, Muslim, and Christian scriptures and stories, fostering a deeper understanding among different faith communities.

Jim's life is a testament to the power of storytelling as a tool for healing, spiritual growth, and fostering understanding in a diverse world. His journey from a family therapist to a spiritual storyteller, death doula, and spiritual guide reflects a lifelong commitment to open-hearted healing and service. His motto, "The right story told in the right way with an open heart can heal wounds and change lives," encapsulates the essence of his life's work, resonating through his numerous programs, workshops, and community engagements. Through every narrative he crafts and every life he touches, Jim Brulé continues to sow seeds of hope, understanding, and compassionate companionship across the myriad paths of human experience.

https://TransformationalStorytelling.org/
IG: LovingTransition

Rebecca Claire Lemaire is a versatile Belgian-British storyteller and is currently based in the Alpujarra mountains in the South of Spain. She tells stories in English, Spanish, and French wherever the wind takes her from Europe to Asia and Africa.

She has lived, studied, and worked in Belgium, the United Kingdom, Indonesia, Arabia (Sultanate of Oman and Kuwait), Morocco, India, France and Spain.

Her passion is to look into people's eyes and travel with them through stories, whether at a festival, in a prison, a yoga school, a Tibetan monastery in the Himalayas, a theatre, or a library. She has played music since she was a child and often uses sounds (flute, kalimba, voice, and drum) to support the stories she tells.

She leads groups into explorations of death and grief through storytelling, conversation, creativity and meditation online, as well as in person. In her community, she is an active member of the group *Morir y Vivir* (Dying and Living), in which the taboo of death is overcome through conversation, practical and spiritual preparation, movies, poetry, and stories. Her practice and training in meditation and as a Reiki healer and teacher support her work with death and grief.

Her work also includes regular performances in Spain and abroad, introductory storytelling courses for teenagers and adults, and training language teachers in storytelling techniques for the classroom.

She obtained a BA in Indonesian and French literature and an MA in Medical Anthropology from SOAS, London, before moving to Asia (Oman and India), where she spent 8 years. She studied music, yoga, Reiki, and meditation in North India before spending two years by Ramana Maharshi's ashram and Arunachala in the South, mostly in silence.

Although she had already been telling stories when teaching yoga, Reiki, English, and meditation, it was when Rebecca returned to Europe that she trained in professional storytelling for three years with Numancia Rojas in Barcelona, Spain. She has also trained with other storytellers from around the world since then and continues to learn from her colleagues.

She says: "Storytelling is a form of communication that goes way beyond words; it is a heart-to-heart interaction, and that is why I love it!"

www.rebeccalemaire.com
IG: rebecca.storyteller

Since we are oral storytellers, we feel it important to give readers the opportunity to experience these stories as we tell them. Therefore, we intend to provide an audio version of this book. In the audio, the stories will not be read exactly as found in the book but rather told. We hope the opportunity to hear us tell these stories—connecting with our voices, the rhythm of the stories, and the occasional music accompanying our storytelling—will give you a fuller experience.

For information about the audiobook and release date, please visit *www.storiesoftheheartbook.com*

www.ingramcontent.com/pod-product-compliance
Lightning Source LLC
LaVergne TN
LVHW011426080426
835512LV00005B/280